Theodore Roosevelt in the Dakota Badlands

An Historical Guide

Clay S. Jenkinson

Published by Dickinson State University
291 Campus Drive
Dickinson, ND 58601
1.800.279.4295
1.701.483.2326

Second Edition

ISBN 0-9786267-0-2

Front cover artwork credits:
Theodore Roosevelt Photograph courtesy of
Theodore Roosevelt Collection, Harvard College Library

Background watercolor [color adjusted] by
Medora von Hoffman de Mores (1856-1921)
Watercolor (1880-1889) courtesy of
State Historical Society of North Dakota
SHSND 1982.29.7

Design by Kelly Noles | Noles Design

Library of Congress Control Number: 2006926985

Theodore Roosevelt in the Dakota Badlands

An Historical Guide

Frequently Asked Questions
About Roosevelt's Adventures
in North Dakota

Second Edition

Clay S. Jenkinson

Published by
The Theodore Roosevelt Center
Dickinson State University

With Support From:
Theodore Roosevelt Medora Foundation
The North Dakota Department of Commerce
North Dakota Cowboy Hall of Fame
Theodore Roosevelt Nature and History Assn.
Theodore Roosevelt National Park
State Historical Society of North Dakota
Badlands Conservation Alliance

Acknowledgments:
Jon Brudvig, Merle Clark, Lillian Crook,
Gary Cummisk, Gia Cummisk, Wallace Dailey,
Darrell Dorgan, Doug Ellison, Jim Fuglie,
Randy Hatzenbuhler, Bruce Kaye, Sharon Kilzer,
Robert Moore, Valerie Naylor, Patricia O'Toole,
Shanna Schoch, Kevin Thompson, Ron Treacy,
Merl Paaverud, Gary Perry, Tweed Roosevelt,
Joe Satrom, David Swenson, Deanna Vickers,
Lee Vickers, Gary White

Dedication

To Sheila Schafer,
like Roosevelt,
forever young

Table of Contents

"I prefer my ranch life to New York life."

Foreward to the Second Edition

It is a sincere pleasure to write this introduction for the second edition of *Theodore Roosevelt in the Dakota Badlands.* President Roosevelt, without question, is one of America's great leaders; and Clay Jenkinson's presentation within this book provides us with an insightful guide for a key time period in Roosevelt's life.

The forces of time and circumstance converge to create the operational environment that every leader must accept as the boundaries of their "arena." Frequently, moments in time, especially moments in history, are viewed as singular events. When these events are isolated from the broader context, we can easily miss the big picture and fail to use the full advantage that can be gained from reflection. The intellectual power of this book resides within the author's ability to present multiple snapshots of key events and historic facts while simultaneously placing them within the context of Roosevelt's life. Each chapter conveys a concise summary of experiences and facts. These selected fragments or data points outline the continuum of development that yielded Roosevelt's bully-pulpit-like character. These frontier experiences form a pattern that is meaningful when viewed through a lens of retrospect that can only be achieved after decades have passed.

We are indebted to Mr. Jenkinson for this scholarly analysis of Roosevelt's time in the Dakota badlands. The years between 1883 and 1887 became defining moments that touched the remaining lifespan of this great American leader. The magical peace of the badlands mixed with the harsh ways of frontier life and the blend of these experiences transformed Roosevelt's soul. He emerged with a sense of purpose. A fire of determination was enkindled within his character. This fire burned for the rest of his life.

To be sure, the four years in the Dakota badlands were a turning point that charted Roosevelt's future destiny. This New York gentleman left the badlands and walked onto the world's stage. His ideas made an unquestionable contribution to the Twentieth Century and his transforming leadership style remains worthy of study today. The energy from his life continues to influence both individually and collectively who we are, where we are going, and who we will become.

In closing, it is indeed a privilege for me to invite you to read and enjoy this new edition of Clay S. Jenkinson's historical guide through Roosevelt's time in the Dakota badlands.

Richard J. McCallum, Ph.D.
President, Dickinson State University

Roosevelt:
The Briefest Life

Theodore Roosevelt was born on October 27, 1858, in New York City. He died on January 6, 1919, at his Sagamore Hill home on Long Island. In the sixty intervening years he lived one of the most strenuous lives in American history.

He was the 26th President of the United States. He ascended to the Presidency on September 14, 1901, when William McKinley died of wounds he received at the hands of an assassin a week earlier. Though Roosevelt pledged to adhere scrupulously to McKinley's policies, he almost immediately set his own course and became perhaps the most active and outspoken President in American history. He was elected in his own right in 1904. He declared that the greatest achievement of his Presidency was the securing of a swath of land in Panama and pressuring Congress into beginning construction on a 51-mile inter-ocean canal. Roosevelt said the building of the Panama Canal was only slightly less important than the

ROOSEVELT'S
BADLANDS TIMELINE

1858
October 27
TR born in New York City

1880
graduates from Harvard College

marries Alice Hathaway Lee

1883
September 7-25
first visit to the Dakota badlands

TR buys the Maltese Cross Ranch

1884
February 14
TR's wife Alice and mother Mittie die in New York

June 9
returns to badlands: establishes Elkhorn Ranch

August-September
hunting trip to Big Horn Mountains

Louisiana Purchase and the annexation of Texas as a milestone in American history.

Roosevelt believed it was his destiny to lead the people of the United States into the Twentieth Century, to expand the powers of the Constitution and especially the Presidency, to make government the guarantor of a "square deal" for all Americans, particularly recent immigrants, the poor, and the inhabitants of great cities. He also believed that the United States must take its place among the great powers of the world, that with the help of a greatly expanded navy it must fill the vacuum being left by the decline of the British Empire. He was an ardent nationalist.

Roosevelt was a successful author, big game hunter, and global adventurer. He was the readingest President of the United States, and also the writingest President. More than thirty books and 150,000 letters and countless articles and columns flowed from his indefatigable pen. Three of his books, *The Naval War of 1812* (1882), the four-volume *Winning of the West* (1889-96) and the *Autobiography* (1913), are regarded as American classics.

He was twice married. His first wife Alice died of Bright's Disease on February 14, 1884. The child of that marriage, Alice Roosevelt Longworth, became one of the most notorious First Daughters in American history.

Roosevelt remarried in December 1886. Edith Carow, who had been his childhood sweetheart, did what she could to manage his Herculean energies and bore Roosevelt five additional children: Theodore (1887), Kermit (1889), Ethel (1891), Archibald (1894), and Quentin (1897). Roosevelt argued that great achievement is wonderful, but it pales in comparison with the joys of family life. "For unflagging interest and enjoyment, a household of children, if things go reasonably well, certainly makes all other forms of success and achievement lose their importance by comparison," he wrote.

After he left the Presidency in 1909, Roosevelt embarked on a year-long safari in East Africa with his son Kermit, in part to give his hapless successor William Howard Taft a chance to establish his own Presidential style. He brought more than 11,000 animal and plant specimens back to the United States for deposit in national museums, particularly the Smithsonian.

In 1914, after the debacle of the Bull Moose campaign, in which Roosevelt received the largest third party vote in American history but only managed to get Woodrow Wilson elected to the Presidency, he undertook (with Kermit) the exploration of one of the last uncharted rivers in South America, today's Rio Roosevelt (or Rio Teodoro). Though Roosevelt declared that it was his "last chance to

1884
December 19
TR organizes Little Missouri River Stockmen's Association

1885
April
probable date of the episode in Mingusville

September
near-duel with Marquis de Mores

1886
March-April
the capture of the boat thieves

July 4
"I like big things" speech in Dickinson

December 2
marries Edith Carow in London, England

1887
April
TR visits Dakota to survey his cattle losses

1888
brief hunting visit

1889
brief hunting visit

1890
September 2-8
TR, Edith, Corinne, Bamie, and others visit Elkhorn Ranch

1891
brief hunting visit

1892
inspection tour of Indian Reservations, hunting at Elkhorn

1893
brief hunting trip

1894
hunting trip

1896
hunting at Elkhorn

1898
sells his remaining cattle interests in Dakota

July 1
TR and Rough Riders assault Kettle and San Juan hills in Cuba

1900
whistle stop in Medora: "here the romance of my life began"

be a boy," the 1500-kilometer journey proved to be an ordeal. Roosevelt lost a quarter of his body mass and nearly died in the South American jungle. He lived six more years, but his health never fully recovered.

When he wasn't seeking manly (and sometimes reckless) adventures, Roosevelt gave his life to public service. He served three terms in the New York State Assembly (1882, 1883, 1884). He ran unsuccessfully for the office of mayor of New York City (1886). He served six years under two Presidents of different parties as U.S. Civil Service Commissioner (1889-95). He was the Police Commissioner of New York City (1895-97). He was the Assistant

TR at Mandan Depot, 1903

Secretary of the Navy (1897-98). And that was the just the beginning!

Roosevelt said the great day of his life was July 1, 1898, when at the front of a "harum scarum" group of rough riders he led the charge up Kettle (and then San Juan) Hill in Cuba, one of the most colorful incidents of the Spanish-American War. Roosevelt's courage in Cuba (and his capacity to write brilliantly about his exploits) made him a national hero and launched him first into the Governorship of New York (1899-1900), then into the Vice Presidency (1901), and finally—by an accident which forestalled his inevitable election in 1904 or 1908—into the Presidency itself.

1901
September 14
TR becomes 26th President of the United States

1903
whistle stop in Medora

1909
March
TR leaves Presidency, embarks on safari in East Africa

1911
whistle stop in Medora

1912
passes through Medora without stopping; the failed Bull Moose campaign

1914
TR explores River of Doubt in South America: "my last chance to be a boy"

1918
whistle stop in Medora

1919
January 6
Roosevelt dies at Oyster Bay, NY

Although Roosevelt is the poster child for the strenuous life, he was a frail and asthmatic boy. Inspired by his father to "make your body," he transformed himself by hard discipline into an uncompromising man of action. The four years he ranched in the badlands of western North Dakota marked the turning point in his life. He came to Dakota a New York dude and he left ready to take on the world.

Roosevelt should be regarded as a conservative reformist. He began his public career as a champion of laissez faire capitalism, but he became steadily more radical as his life unfolded. Critics accused him of co-opting the Progressive Movement's agenda, but Roosevelt believed that he was both purifying the reform movement of its socialist and sentimental extremism and at the same time saving corporate capitalism by insuring that it behaved according to minimal standards of decency and fair play. By 1910 he was an economic radical. The views he espoused between 1910 and his death in 1919 essentially anticipated his fifth cousin Franklin Roosevelt's New Deal.

Roosevelt threw himself unhesitatingly into every arena of existence. His energies, his passions, his utterances, his opinions, and his appetites were all larger than life. His friend and critic Henry Adams said Roosevelt reminded him of the God of the scholastic philosophers: "pure act."

When Roosevelt died in his sleep on January 6, 1919, his son Archie cabled the others with the message, "The old lion is dead."

What Is Special about the Year 1883?

Theodore Roosevelt visited the badlands of Dakota Territory for the first time, September 7-25, 1883.

That same year, the Marquis de Mores (Antoine-Amédée-Marie-Vincent-Amat Manca de Vallombrosa) took up residence in the Dakota badlands. He was far wealthier and more entrepreneurial than Roosevelt. When he could not convince the citizens of Little Missouri to cooperate with his grandiose schemes, he crossed the river and created an entirely new town, which he named for his wife Medora von Hoffman.

The population of the United States was 50,155,783. There were 38 states. The President was Chester Arthur, who had ascended to that office when James Garfield was assassinated in 1881.

In 1883 the world's first rodeo was held in Pecos, Texas. The first vaudeville theater was opened in Boston, Massachusetts.

De Mores and Roosevelt would spend an almost identical amount of time in the badlands of Dakota. Both ceased to be active residents in 1887, after one of the most destructive winters in the recorded history of the northern Great Plains.

1883 was the year that the Northern Pacific Railroad, chartered by Congress in 1864 to connect Lake Superior and the Puget Sound, was substantially finished. In fact, a special commemorative train passed through the Dakota badlands just one day before Roosevelt made his first appearance. The train included former President Ulysses S. Grant, NP president Henry Villard, and scores of others. Given Roosevelt's social connections, his fierce ambition to be wherever the action was, and the coincidence of his trip to

Dakota just when the golden spike ceremony occurred, it is strange that he did not talk his way onto that previous VIP train.

1883 was also the year of the last great buffalo hunt on the northern plains. At the beginning of the year there were well more than 10,000 buffalo still grazing on the northern range. By the time Roosevelt arrived in Dakota, professional buffalo hunters and Sioux (Lakota) warriors had all but wiped out the herd.

The Brooklyn Bridge opened in 1883.

A group of five civil rights cases were decided by the U.S. Supreme Court in 1883, effectively voiding the Fourteenth Amendment's equal protection clause for African-Americans. The court upheld Jim Crow laws that disenfranchised black men.

Hunkpapa leader Sitting Bull was permitted to take up permanent residence on the Standing Rock Indian Reservation in 1883, after a long sojourn in "Grandmother's Land" (Canada) following the wiping out of Custer at the Little Bighorn on June 25, 1876. Sitting Bull lived on the reservation, which straddles today's North Dakota-South Dakota border, until his assassination on December 15, 1890.

In 1883, Texas longhorns began to arrive in large numbers into northern Dakota Territory. The grangers of Texas discovered that longhorns thrived on the northern range, in spite of the brutal winters. The first Texas-derived ranches were formed in the upper (southern) Little Missouri River Valley not long before Roosevelt arrived on the scene.

The Mayo Clinic was opened in Rochester, Minnesota.

On January 16, 1883, the U.S. Civil Service Commission was established. Roosevelt, who believed ardently in good government, would serve as a U.S. Civil Service Commissioner from 1889-95.

The *Ladies' Home Journal* published its first issue on February 16, 1883.

America's greatest writer Samuel Clemens published *Life on the Mississippi* in 1883. Scottish novelist and poet Robert Louis Stevenson published the young person's classic *Treasure Island.* German philosopher Frederick Nietzsche published *Also Sprach Zarathustra* in which he declared, "God is dead."

Karl Marx died in London. Richard Wagner died in Venice. The Russian novelist Ivan Turgenev died in Bougival, in France.

On October 4, the Orient Express began service between Paris and Turkey. The United States and Canada adopted standard time zones to facilitate railroad traffic.

In 1883 the state of Mississippi established the nation's first state college for women. Roosevelt was a quasi-advocate of women's rights all of his life, and more so after he left the Presidency in 1909. In 1912 he would receive the first electoral vote cast by a woman in American history.

On May 17, Buffalo Bill Cody's first Wild West Show premiered in Omaha, Nebraska. When Roosevelt organized the Rough Riders to liberate Cuba in the Spanish-American War in 1898, Cody wished to join Roosevelt and his volunteer regiment of cowboys and Indians, but he could not extricate himself from his Wild West touring contract.

On August 27, the island volcano Krakatoa erupted in Indonesia. The resulting tidal waves killed 36,417 people in Java and Sumatra.

Theodore Roosevelt was, of course, aware of all of these events. He was one of the best-informed and widely-read Americans of his time. The great stir of the world's affairs interested him deeply. But what he really wanted in the early fall of 1883 was to kill one of the last of America's buffalo.

He was 24 years old.

What Sort of Man Was Roosevelt in 1883?

He was young and frail. He had recently endured a bout of cholera morbus. He had suffered all of his life from debilitating asthma. As recently as his last year at Harvard, his physician had warned him that he had a weak heart and a frail constitution and that he should not expect to live a full life.

He was not then the barrel-chested, tending-towards-corpulent man that he had become by the time he took the oath of office as 26th President of the United States. In 1883, he was a thin, bespectacled, somewhat insubstantial young man, defined more by his natty clothes, his Harvard education, his class consciousness, and his falsetto voice than by his actual deeds, which were surprisingly hectic for such a frail and refined eastern aristocrat. Even as late as 1885, A.T. Packard of the *Bad Lands Cow Boy* suggested that the easterner was merely "playing at cowboy."

He was an extremely privileged young man. He could afford to dabble in ranch and cowboy life. He first appeared in the Little Missouri River Valley wearing a designer suit of cowboy duds, a knife purchased at Tiffany's, and monogrammed spurs. He came from a prominent New York family. His father, Theodore senior, had been a widely admired philanthropist. Roosevelts had access to all the fruits of life as they were understood in the post-Civil War period. Roosevelt's accent was touched by pretentiousness honed at Harvard.

One of his badlands acquaintances said, "You could have spanned his waist with your two thumbs and fingers."

He was a rising star in New York reform politics. First elected to the New York State Legislature in 1881, he had distinguished himself for his shrill political righteousness. Earlier in 1883, he narrowly missed becoming Speaker. He had cast his lot with politics at a time when the social elites turned away from the political arena in disgust. He was already a loud, opinionated, and pugnacious political warrior.

He was married. In fact, his wife Alice Hathaway Lee was four months pregnant. He adored his wife, called her "precious," "angel," "saint," and "little darling," and indulged her in every way possible.

Young Roosevelt was a serious intellectual. It seemed natural to him to carry a book with him at all times, and to sit apart from others reading it at leisure moments. All of his life Roosevelt was a tireless reader. He had already published an important book, begun while he was still a student at Harvard, on the *Naval War of 1812*. He regarded himself as a man of letters and he was, in the mid-1880s, seriously considering making his career as a writer. At Harvard he had wanted to become a naturalist, until he became disenchanted with Harvard's insistence on laboratory work rather than field observation. He knew the flora and fauna of America. He had a particular fascination with birds.

He was, he later admitted, still afraid of many things. "There were all kinds of things I was afraid of at first, ranging from grizzly bears to 'mean' horses and gunfighters; but by acting as if I was not afraid I gradually ceased to be afraid."

In 1883 Roosevelt was already a committed hunter. The big game phase of his life was about to begin. His mastery of hunting had more to do with doggedness and determination than with natural skill. His eyesight was remarkably poor. Experienced frontiersmen shook their heads that so nearly blind a man would try his luck in an arena that required a sharp eye. At first they made fun of him. Soon they would be rather impressed.

He was willful and notional. He was aware that the American frontier was fast disappearing. He was convinced that the frontier experience had been the defining factor in the shaping of American character and national identity. He was determined to get his taste of life on the frontier while it was still possible. He felt righteous distaste for the dissipation and ennui that characterized the urban social elite of the United States as the Nineteenth Century closed.

He thirsted for authentic experience. And he wanted very much to kill a buffalo.

How Do You Pronounce "Roosevelt?"

It's ROSE-a-velt not RUSE-a-velt. Roosevelt was firm about this. He also detested being called Teddy. "Teddy" was a term of endearment used by his first wife Alice Hathaway Lee. His grief was so great after her death in February 1884 that he could not bear to hear himself called by her pet name. He also considered "Teddy" a boy's, not a man's, name.

During his Dakota years, Roosevelt insisted upon being called Mr. Roosevelt. In 1884, when his wagoner Norman Lebo called him Theodore, Roosevelt rebuked him severely.

Picture this:

Roosevelt's Arrival in Little Missouri

Theodore Roosevelt arrives at the tiny village of Little Missouri on the western edge of Dakota Territory around 3 a.m. on the night of September 7-8, 1883. According to his own account, he is the only passenger to disembark at Little Missouri that night. The rail stop, such as it is, offers no amenities and no waiting platform.

Roosevelt had arrived in the Dakota badlands in the dark. This was his first visit to the true West. Though he may have experienced the brokenness of the countryside in silhouette as the Northern Pacific steam train chugged from Belfield down into the badlands, it would not be until after dawn on September 8 that he will gaze on the weirdness of the Little Missouri River Valley for the first time.

Roosevelt carries his duffle bag and guns to a ramshackle hotel north of the tracks.

He knocks on the door of the Pyramid Park Hotel, partly owned by Roosevelt's New York friend Henry Gorringe and operated by a man named "Captain" Frank Moore.

Moore leads Roosevelt upstairs to the "bull-pen," an un-partitioned loft over which fourteen cots are scattered. Thirteen of them are occupied—by the kind of men who drifted around the cattle and railroad frontier in the 1880s. Some of them, surely, are snoring. One cot is empty. Its linens are doubtful. Roosevelt takes it. It is Hobson's choice.

In the morning, when breakfast is announced, the inhabitants of the bull-pen unceremoniously stampede down the stairs of the Pyramid Park in pursuit of grub. When Roosevelt at last reaches the wash basin, its waters are foul and the seamless sack towel is sodden and filthy.

Thus the New York dude, the Harvard-educated aristocrat who is accustomed to using the finest soaps and being shaved by a professional barber, gets his first taste of the democracy of the frontier.

There is no evidence that Roosevelt found these experiences anything but "dee-lightful." He had come west to immerse himself in some authentic frontier experiences before the march of civilization swallowed up the last of America's untamed country. He had not come west to remake the wild country, but to soak it up and take it as it actually was.

He strolls six or seven miles that morning, to get some exercise after five days aboard the train from New York, and then begins his search for a local hunting guide.

The romance of Roosevelt's life has begun.

Why Did Roosevelt Choose the Badlands of Dakota Territory and Not Somewhere Else?

Three reasons. First, he had made the acquaintance in New York of a man named Commodore Henry Gorringe, a retired naval officer. Gorringe was the man who brought Cleopatra's Needle (the 71-foot, 200 ton ancient Egyptian obelisk) to New York City in 1880.

In 1883, Gorringe had purchased the abandoned military cantonment on the western edge of the village of Little Missouri with the idea of making it a hunting lodge. Roosevelt met Gorringe in May, 1883, at the Free Trade Club in New York. Gorringe invited Roosevelt to join him in a trip to the Dakota badlands in the late summer of 1883. Roosevelt accepted the invitation. But for unknown reasons Gorringe backed out of the trip at the last minute. Roosevelt decided to go anyway.

Second, the Little Missouri River Valley was comparatively easy to get to. All Roosevelt had to do was take the train from New York to Chicago and then St. Paul, switch to the Northern Pacific, and then ride the NP to Bismarck and eventually the village of Little Missouri. It was, by Nineteenth Century standards, an easy five-day railroad journey. Roosevelt could get right to the place he wanted to go by rail, without any need to make connections with a stage line, or hire someone to guide him to a place remote from the transportation infrastructure. Had he wanted to hunt in the Black Hills, for example, he would have had to endure a long stagecoach ride from Bismarck or Cheyenne. The hunting grounds of Dakota Territory were right outside the Northern Pacific "platform," such as it was.

Third, there was a Dakota badlands boom in 1883.

In 1871, Hiram Latham had published *Trans-Missouri Stock Raising; the Pasture Lands of North America; Winter Grazing.* James S. Brisbin's *The Beef Bonanza; or How to Get Rich on the Plains* was published in 1881.

New York, Paris, and London newspapers had been reporting a buzz of activity on the northern plains. Some of Roosevelt's Harvard friends had already invested in ranches in Dakota Territory. Roosevelt himself had invested $10,000 in a Wyoming ranch operated by a Harvard classmate. Suddenly it was fashionable for aristocrats on both sides of the Atlantic to have a cattle ranch somewhere in those parts of the American West recently wrested from American Indians. In 1883, the first great rush of Texas longhorns reached northern Dakota Territory.

Roosevelt himself had chosen to hunt in Dakota Territory after conversations with Howard Eaton of Pittsburgh, and Gorringe of New York. Roosevelt ventured to one of America's last frontiers in 1883, but it was far from unknown in the elite social circles in which Roosevelt traveled.

Did Medora Exist When Roosevelt First Came to Dakota Territory in 1883?

Yes. The Marquis de Mores christened the new village on April 1, 1883, in honor of his wife Medora von Hoffman. This was five months before Roosevelt made his first appearance. The village of Little Missouri was still in existence. It had not yet been eclipsed by the Marquis' Medora. The Northern Pacific Railroad continued to stop at Little Missouri until 1884.

By early 1884, the upstart village of Medora could boast of having 84 buildings and a population of about 250. Businesses included five saloons, three hotels, a newspaper office, a laundry, a barber shop, a blacksmith shop, and a photographic gallery, in addition to general stores. The ebullient de Mores predicted that Medora would soon become the Omaha of the northern plains.

Roosevelt called Medora an "excessively unattractive little hamlet," but it was nevertheless his western home town for four years.

The killing winter of 1886-87, coupled with de Mores' impulsive decision to fulfill his dreams elsewhere, brought the village of Medora into rapid decline. De Mores' packing plant closed for good in 1887. Fire destroyed the office of the *Bad Lands Cow Boy* in January 1887. Editor A.T. Packard departed. By the spring of 1887 only a saloon, a boardinghouse, and the general store survived.

Medora's brief Nineteenth Century moment had come and gone.

Medora 1885: The de Mores slaughterhouse in the center background.

Where Did Roosevelt Stay When He First Arrived in the Badlands?

Roosevelt arrived on the train about 3 a.m. on the night of September 7-8, 1883. The train stopped in the village of Little Missouri, sometimes called Comba, on the west bank of the Little Missouri River. Roosevelt spent the rest of that first night at the Pyramid Park Hotel.

The next day he managed to hire the reluctant Joe Ferris to serve as his hunting guide, borrowed from the formidable and shifty-eyed E.G. Paddock a rifle strong enough to kill a buffalo, and traveled seven miles south of Little Missouri in a buck wagon to the Maltese Cross Ranch, also known as the Chimney Butte Ranch, occupied by William Merrifield and Ferris' brother Sylvane. There he spent his second night in the badlands (September 8). Although Merrifield and Sylvane Ferris were not at first impressed by the New York dude, they gained some appreciation when he insisted on sleeping on the floor rather than displace them from their beds.

For the rest of his buffalo hunt, Roosevelt headquartered at the cabin of Gregor and Lincoln Lang, recent Scottish immigrants who were managing the investment of an English capitalist named Sir John Pender. Lang's cabin (the first of three the Langs occupied in the badlands) was located at the mouth of Little Cannonball Creek, just north of Pretty Butte, near today's Marmarth, North Dakota.

After a ten-day hunt, Roosevelt returned to the Pyramid Park Hotel on the nights of September 22-23, 1883, before embarking for St. Paul and then New York City.

Roosevelt did not actually take possession of the Chimney Butte Ranch headquarters until his return to the Little Missouri River Valley in June 1884.

How Did People in Dakota React to Roosevelt?

At first they were amused, skeptical, and sometimes derisive. Roosevelt cut a somewhat ridiculous figure with his designer buckskins and his Tiffany's knife, his falsetto voice and Harvard accent. He sensed this himself.

In his *Autobiography*, he wrote, "When I went among strangers I always had to spend twenty-four hours in living down the fact that I wore spectacles, remaining as long as I could judiciously deaf to any side remarks about 'four eyes' unless it became evident that my being quiet was misconstrued and that it was better to bring matters to a head at once."

To Henry Cabot Lodge he provided a romantic portrait of himself, on August 12, 1884. "You would be amused to see me, in my broad sombrero hat, fringed and beaded buckskin shirt, horse hide chaparajos or riding trousers, and cowhide boots, with braided bridle and silver spurs."

In the course of their ten-day buffalo hunt in 1883, Joe Ferris realized that there was something irrepressible in Roosevelt's character. Ferris said, "I liked him from the start. He struck me as a quiet sort of man, easy to get along with."

Scotsman Gregor Lang realized Roosevelt's greatness in the week of late evening conversations he had with TR about ranching, the West, and American politics. When Roosevelt and Joe Ferris finally drove north towards the village of Little Missouri, carrying the head of Roosevelt's buffalo in Ferris's buckboard, on September 22, 1883, Gregor Lang turned to his son and said, "There goes the most remarkable man I ever met."

The Roosevelt who returned to civilization in 1887 was a very different figure from the young man who arrived in the badlands in September 1883.

Little Missouri rancher Frank Roberts said, "He was rather a slim-lookin' fellow when he came out here, but after he lived out here... his build got wider and heavier... he got to be lookin' more like a rugged man."

Upon Roosevelt's return to life in the East, one of his Harvard classmates wrote, "I recall my astonishment the first time I saw him, after the lapse of several years, to find him with the neck of a Titan and with broad shoulders and stalwart chest, instead of the city-bred, slight young friend I had known earlier."

The greatest praise Roosevelt received from a resident of the Little Missouri River Valley came from Lincoln Lang.

It was like a scene out of a Laura Ingalls Wilder novel. From his bed in the cabin, young Lincoln listened to his father and Roosevelt talk deep into the night, after each exhausting day of Roosevelt's buffalo hunt. Undoubtedly he drifted off before the conversations were finished, but he heard enough to form a lifelong judgment of Roosevelt. In *Ranching with Roosevelt*, he wrote, "It was listening to those talks after supper in the old shack on the Cannonball, that I first came to understand that the Lord made the earth for all of us, and not for a chosen few."

What Happened to the Buffalo That Roosevelt Shot in North Dakota?

It's on display in the North Room at Sagamore Hill, Roosevelt's home at Oyster Bay on Long Island.

After shooting the buffalo on September 20, 1883, Roosevelt returned the next day to decapitate the critter and strip the hide off the carcass. That night Roosevelt, Joe Ferris, and Gregor and Lincoln Lang feasted on the prime cuts of the buffalo at the Langs' cabin on Little Cannonball Creek. "The flesh of the bull tasted uncommonly good to us for we had been without fresh meat for a week; and until a healthy, active man has been without it for some little time, he does not know how positively and almost painfully hungry for flesh he becomes, no matter how much farinaceous food he may have."

Roosevelt took the buffalo head with him when he traveled east on September 25. He stopped in Bismarck to get it mounted, or at least prepared for taxidermy in New York.

The trophy has been on display at Sagamore Hill for more than a century. Also on display from the Dakota years are branding irons of the Maltese Cross and Elkhorn ranches, spurs, Roosevelt's Sharps .45 and his Winchester Model 1876. Other animal trophies (probably from Dakota) include mule deer antlers and the heads of pronghorn antelopes.

Roosevelt's Tiffany's knife is now in the family's private collection. His buckskin shirt has, alas, disappeared.

What Other Animals Did Roosevelt Hunt in Dakota Territory?

Roosevelt spoke of "seven kinds of plains game—bear, buffalo, elk, bighorn, antelope, blacktail or whitetail deer."

By December 14, 1884, Roosevelt had successfully hunted at least one of everything on his list. Deer and elk were easy. Roosevelt hunted both mule deer and white tailed deer, of course. Buffalo are not hard to kill; the problem was finding one to kill. That was September 20, 1883.

Roosevelt got his first pronghorn antelope in June 1884 on his journey to Mrs. Maddox's cabin east of the badlands. He got his first grizzly bear on September 13, 1884, in the Big Horn Mountains of northern Wyoming.

The last of the big game animals on his list was the bighorn sheep. He bagged one finally on December 14, 1884, in the vicinity of Bullion Butte, south of Medora. It was bitterly cold (ten below zero) and the rough slopes of the butte had become dangerous with crusted snow and ice. He shot a ram while hunting on foot the second day out. Later he wrote, "Still-hunting the bighorn is always a toilsome and laborious task.... If a man keeps at it, it is bound to make him both hardy and resolute; to strengthen his muscles and fill out his lungs."

How Much Land Did Roosevelt Actually Own in the Little Missouri River Valley?

None. He squatted on many thousands of acres, some surrounding the Maltese and some surrounding the Elkhorn ranch headquarters. Roosevelt paid taxes on his capital investment in the cattle industry, but he never owned an acre of Dakota property.

Most of the inhabitants of the badlands during this period actually owned no land. It was open range, recently taken from its Indian sovereigns, not yet deeded out under the Homestead Act (1862), the Timber Culture Act (1873) or the Desert Lands Act (1877). Most of it was owned by the government of the United States. Some of it comprised the gigantic swath of land (40,000,000 acres) granted to the Northern Pacific Railroad as incentive to build the transcontinental rail line, not yet disposed of by the NP. When the Marquis de Mores began to obtain actual title to acreage in the badlands, he was regarded as a nuisance who was violating the unwritten code of open range and informal land tenancy.

In 1884, Roosevelt paid someone, perhaps a hunter, perhaps an existing rancher, $400 to extinguish a rival claim on the Elkhorn site. This was not a means of actually buying land, but rather of pre-empting an existing squatter.

In the book he wrote about his ranch experiences, *Hunting Trips of a Ranchman*, 1885, Roosevelt acknowledged that squatter cattlemen did not hold legal claims to the lands on which they grazed their herds.

"The cattle-men... keep herds and build houses on the land; yet I would not for a moment debar settlers from the right of entry to the cattle country, though their coming in means in the end the destruction of us and our industry. For we ourselves, and the life that we lead, will shortly pass away from the plains as completely as the red and white hunters who have vanished from before our herds."

In other words, Roosevelt acknowledged that when farmers with valid land deeds entered the western reaches of Dakota Territory, squatter ranchers would have no choice but to acknowledge the newcomers' superior claims and withdraw from the land.

In the meantime, as Roosevelt wrote in *Hunting Trips of a Ranchman*, a rancher was by custom entitled to a swath of land four miles upriver and four miles downriver from his headquarters and indefinitely in a perpendicular direction.

How Much Time Did Roosevelt Actually Spend in North Dakota?

A little over a year total. His significant residencies were spread over a four-year period between September 7, 1883, and December 5, 1887.

In 1883, he spent approximately 21 days in the badlands. In 1884, he made four trips to Dakota (and the Big Horn Mountains) for a total of approximately 73 days. In 1885 he made two sustained trips to his Dakota ranches. The total appears to have been 87 days that year.

In 1886, he made one long and a number of shorter visits, totaling approximately 133 days. The period between March 19 and July 8 was his longest sustained visit to the Little Missouri River Valley.

In 1887, after the disastrous winter, Roosevelt made two visits to his western ranches. The first, April 9-20, reminded him of just how much he and every other rancher had lost. The second, between November 1 and December 5, 1887, was a hunting trip. The total for 1887 is approximately 45 days.

The total for all of these visits, between 1883 and 1887, comes to something like 359 days.

Roosevelt continued to visit the Dakota badlands to hunt almost every year until 1896. Thereafter, he visited North Dakota six more times, always to advance his political agenda, and never for more than a couple of days. He last visited the badlands on October 6, 1918, just a few months before his death.

For some reason, Roosevelt was sensitive about the amount of time he spent in Dakota Territory. Although he was incapable of lying outright, he frequently exaggerated when describing his exploits, and for some reason he led the world to believe that he had spent more time in Dakota than he actually did. In Fargo in 1910, Roosevelt said, "It is twenty-seven years since I first punched cattle on the Little Missouri, where I lived for the major part of seven years, and off and on for nearly fifteen years."

How Much Actual Work Did Roosevelt Do Among Cattle?

More than you might think. He wanted desperately to be accepted by the ranchers and cowboys of the American West, so he threw himself unhesitatingly into the life of the range. He refused to consider any labor beneath his dignity, however dirty, dangerous, or unpleasant it was. He never complained, never willingly called attention to himself, never was first in the grub line or last up in the morning.

Because his eyesight was so poor, Roosevelt never became adept with the lasso. His horsemanship was more dogged than graceful. He tended therefore to do the most basic work of the roundup, riding the perimeter of the herds, often working both day and night shifts, and wrestling calves to the ground for branding.

On one occasion he was in the saddle for forty hours straight, on five different horses. Before that marathon work stint was over, Roosevelt helped stop a stampede.

In June 1884 he participated in the first-ever general roundup in the Little Missouri River Valley. In 1885 he participated in the spring roundup for 32 straight days, along with 60 other men, more than 300 horses, and thousands of cattle. In five weeks he rode more than a thousand miles up and down the Little Missouri River.

Roosevelt rode whatever horse was put in front of him. He was frequently thrown by the wild ones. He broke ribs and the point of his shoulder in the course of his roundup adventures, but he forced himself never to miss a work call. Lincoln Lang recalled that Roosevelt once drew a mean bucking horse. He "gave us all an exhibition of the stuff he was made of.... He had his grip and like grim death he hung on... hat, glasses, six-shooter, everything unanchored about him took the count. But there was no breaking his grip.... he stuck." Roosevelt's account was more comical. "I rode him all the way from the tip of his ear to the end of his tail."

One long-time cowboy concluded, "That four-eyed maverick has sand in his craw a-plenty."

To his closest friend Henry Cabot Lodge, he wrote, "I have been three weeks on the roundup and have worked as hard as any of the cowboys... Yesterday I was eighteen hours in the saddle—from 4 a.m. to 10 p.m.—having half an hour each for dinner and tea. I can now do cowboy work pretty well."

In 1886 Roosevelt wrote, "We breakfast at three every morning, and work from sixteen to eighteen hours a day, counting night guard; so I get pretty sleepy; but I feel strong as a bear."

Roosevelt did all this hard and dangerous work without complaining, but he also read a good deal during leisure moments, and he listened carefully to the stories, the poetry, and the songs of the cowboys who rode night guard. Later in his life, he encouraged the folklorist John Lomax to record as much cowboy culture as possible. In fact, Roosevelt wrote the preface to Lomax's 1910 book *Cowboy Songs and Other Frontier Ballads*.

"*A great many young fellows have an idea that the life of a ranchman, from its very hardships and risks, must have a certain romantic attraction to it... but the romance evaporates after a couple of months spent in a muddy dugout with no amusements whatsoever, and on a steady diet of rancid bacon, sodden biscuits, and alkali water.*"

Roosevelt
Harper's Weekly, January 1886

Picture this:

The Affair in Mingusville

A rough and tumble frontier hotel on the Northern Pacific line just inside Montana.

The tenderfoot Roosevelt has been riding the range in search of strayed horses. It is too late to get back to his ranches on the Little Missouri River, so he takes a room at Nolan's Hotel in Mingusville (since 1895 known as Wibaux, Montana). The tenderfoot is informed that the only restaurant in Mingusville is in the saloon downstairs. Roosevelt, who is essentially a teetotaler, reluctantly makes his way to the saloon. Inside there is pandemonium. A drunken gunslinger is shooting up the bar and menacing the clientele. He has been using the clock for target practice.

The other patrons in the bar are "wearing the kind of smile worn by men who are making believe to like what they don't like."

The gunslinger, "not a 'bad man' of the really dangerous type," but nevertheless "an objectionable creature," notices the bespectacled dude Roosevelt as he tries to slip as unobtrusively as possible into a corner table behind the stove.

Now the trouble begins.

"Four eyes is going to treat."

Roosevelt laughs in a good-natured way "and got behind the stove and sat down, thinking to escape notice."

The bully persists. "Though I tried to pass it off as a jest this merely made him more offensive, and he stood leaning over me, a gun in each hand, using very foul language." The ruffian again insists that Roosevelt is standing drinks for the whole bar.

Theodore Roosevelt has had enough.

Roosevelt studied boxing at Harvard. He is a rather skilled pugilist. He is, moreover, sober. He notices that the drunken gunslinger's feet are rather too close together and that his center of gravity, therefore, is by no means adequate.

Says Roosevelt, "Well, if I've got to, I've got to."

"As I rose, I struck quick and hard with my right just to one side of the point of his jaw, hitting with my left as I straightened out, and then again with my right. He fired the guns, but I do not know whether this was merely a convulsive action of his hands or whether he was trying to shoot me." Surely Roosevelt hopes it was the latter.

Down goes the ruffian. Down goes the gunslinger, like a sack of potatoes.

Fortunately, in falling backward from the force of Roosevelt's punches, the gunslinger hits his head on the bar and is knocked cold.

"It was not a case in which one could afford to take chances, and if he had moved I was about to drop on his ribs with my knees; but he was senseless."

Roosevelt disarms the ruffian. Suddenly, the bar patrons who had been cowering and doing everything in their power to conciliate the gunman when Roosevelt entered the saloon, grow brave and "loud in their denunciation of him."

The troublemaker is hustled out of the bar and thrown into a shed.

"When my assailant came to, he went down to the station and left on a freight [train]."

Roosevelt finishes his meal and goes back to his room. Word travels fast in the badlands. The punkinlily from New York is not to be trifled with. He's got pluck and courage, and he's outstanding in a crisis.

"Roosevelt was regarded by the cowboys as a good deal of a joke until after the saloon incident. After that it was different," said railroad official Frank Greene, years later.

Historians are not quite sure just when this incident occurred. Edmund Morris, in *The Rise of Theodore Roosevelt*, places it in the late summer of 1884. Hermann Hagedorn, the author of *Roosevelt in the Badlands*, prefers June 1884. Morris dismisses this as logistically impossible. Carleton Putnam, *Theodore Roosevelt: The Formative Years*, chooses April 1885. Contemporaries, including Pierre Wibaux of Mingusville, agree that the incident occurred "shortly after July 1884." Unless new evidence surfaces, it is only safe to conclude that the incident occurred sometime between June 1884 and June 1885.

How Did Roosevelt's Ranches Get Their Names?

Roosevelt's first Dakota ranch was headquartered seven miles south of the village of Little Missouri on the east bank of the Little Missouri River. The most prominent feature in the area was a sandstone outcropping called Chimney Butte. Roosevelt did not create the ranch. He bought out the interests of Minnesota investors by the names of W. L. Hawley and Hiram B. Wadsworth. It was those capitalists who had chosen what is called the Maltese Cross brand for the Chimney Butte ranch. It is not clear whether they designed the brand as a Maltese Cross or rather that the brand's resemblance to a Maltese Cross led the ranch community to adopt that name. In his *Autobiography*, Roosevelt said it was locally known as the "maltee cross," "as the general impression along the Little Missouri was that 'maltese' must be plural."

In point of fact, the brand of the Chimney Butte ranch was a Jerusalem, not a Maltese Cross. More precisely still, the brand is known technically as a Cross Potent, which is often coupled with the Jerusalem Cross.

Roosevelt simply accepted the existing nomenclature—the brand would have been registered with the Territorial Agriculture Department.

Roosevelt's other ranch bore the stamp of his own personality and his personal exploration of the Little Missouri River Valley. When he returned to Dakota in June 1884 after the death of his wife and mother in New York, Roosevelt determined to create a second ranch somewhere remote from the traffic lanes of the Medora-Little Missouri area, and well away from the railroad line.

A man named Howard Eaton, who had been in the Valley since 1879, and who had his own ranch at the mouth of Big Beaver Creek, appears to have suggested the general location to Roosevelt. Sometime around June 20, 1884, Roosevelt rode out alone north of Medora in search of good grazing land that was not yet claimed. He found a perfect ranch site 35 miles north of Medora.

On one of his subsequent visits there, he found the interlocked horns of two bull elk, who had been fighting when their horns got tangled. They had starved to death on the spot.

This was just the sort of symbol most likely to impress a big game hunter, lover of nature, Darwinist, and advocate of the strenuous life. Roosevelt immediately seized upon the name, and created a brand that represented, in very simple lines, the horn of an elk.

In short, Roosevelt *adopted* the Chimney Butte Ranch and had a modest cabin built for himself there. But he *invented* the Elkhorn Ranch: he chose the location, gave it a name, brought in his own management team from Maine, and had a house built there to his specifications of comfort (particularly the veranda). It is clear from all that he wrote about his Dakota experiences that he regarded the Elkhorn as his true western home. It was there that he wrote his badlands prose. It was there that he took Edith in 1890.

Did Roosevelt Actually Build Either of His Badlands Cabins?

No. The Maltese Cross Ranch was already well established when he purchased it in September 1883. In fact, W. L. Hawley and Hiram B. Wadsworth of Minnesota are credited with creating one of the first ranches in the badlands at

Chimney Butte. The existing living quarters, made of vertical timbers, were inadequate for Roosevelt's needs, so his ranch supervisors Sylvane Ferris and Bill Merrifield built him a larger and more comfortable cabin between his departure in September 1883 and his return in June 1884. This is the famous Roosevelt cabin that now sits on the grounds of the visitor center at Theodore Roosevelt National Park. It had three rooms, plus an attic, under a steeply pitched roof. The old vertical-post cabin at the Maltese Cross Ranch became the stable.

Roosevelt played a small role in the construction of the Elkhorn cabin. It was an eight-room, 60 by 30 foot wooden house, with a veranda fronting east towards the Little Missouri River.

In the *Autobiography* Roosevelt freely admits, "The Elkhorn ranch house was built mainly by Sewall and Dow, who, like most men from the Maine woods, were mighty with the ax." Roosevelt spent no more than a handful of days working at the construction site. William Sewall and Wilmot Dow were acquaintances of Roosevelt's,

Roosevelt's Maltese Cross Ranch South of Medora

professional lumbermen from Maine, whom he had persuaded to move to Dakota to manage the Elkhorn Ranch on shares. They built the Elkhorn cabin. Roosevelt helped a little.

In the late fall of 1884, Roosevelt helped Sewall and Dow cut down cottonwood trees for the cabin. He recorded a comic evaluation of his capacity as a lumberman. "I heard some one ask Dow what the total cut had been, and Dow, not realizing that I was within hearing, answered: 'Well, Bill cut down fifty-three, I cut forty-nine, and the boss he beavered down seventeen.'"

Roosevelt seems to have regarded house construction as a routine craft, not very interesting to a man with a thirst for adventure. He preferred to spend his time in the badlands either hunting or writing books, and he left the building projects to his hired men, who were better at it anyway.

The Elkhorn cabin has entirely disappeared, though boards from the structure are rumored to grace several ranch houses in the Little Missouri River Valley. The Chimney Butte cabin, much modified and several times restored, still exists.

How Much Did Roosevelt Grieve for Alice in the Badlands?

Roosevelt's first wife Alice died suddenly on Valentine's Day, 1884. She was 22 years old. His mother died on the same day, in the same house, at the age of 49. Needless to say, Roosevelt was devastated. He finished up his legislative work in Albany, attended the Republican National Convention in Chicago, and then hastened to the Dakota badlands to bury himself in physical work and solitude.

The evidence we have suggests that the summer of 1884 was a very difficult time for Roosevelt.

Rancher Margaret Roberts later remembered him as "sad and quiet" during this time. Historians have noted the frequency with which he uses the word "lonely," in the writings of this period.

"Nowhere, not even at sea," he wrote, "does a man feel more lonely than when riding over the far reaching, seemingly never-ending plains. Their very vastness and... their melancholy monotony have a strong fascination for me."

It would be easy to quote many more such moments of melancholy.

During the summer of 1884, Roosevelt confided his sorrow to his hired man William Sewall at the Elkhorn Ranch. Sewall observed that Roosevelt was "very melancholy at times." At one point, in the depths of his grief, Roosevelt said he felt he had no reason to live on. "You have your child to live for," Sewall said. "She would be just as well off without me," Roosevelt replied, "Her aunt [Bamie] can take care of her a good deal better than I can." Sewall responded, "You won't always feel as you do now and you won't always be willing to stay here and drive cattle."

The two greatest expressions of his grief were a brief written tribute to Alice, written in August 1884, and a conversation he had in the remote Big Horn Mountains with his ranch manager William Merrifield.

Just before he left on the Big Horn trek, Roosevelt wrote the only memorial he would ever write for his first wife. It was for a small collection of newspaper clippings and tributes to his wife that he had privately printed to be distributed to family and friends.

> In Memory of My Darling Wife
>
> She was beautiful in face and form, and lovelier still in spirit; as a flower she grew, and as a fair young flower she died. Her life had always been in the sunshine; there had never come to her a single great sorrow; and none ever knew her who did not love and revere her for her bright, sunny temper and her saintly unselfishness. Fair, pure, and joyous as a maiden; loving, tender, and happy as a young wife; when she had just become a mother, when her life seemed to be but just begun, and when the years seemed so bright before her—then by a strange and terrible fate, death came to her.
>
> And when my heart's dearest died, the light went from my life forever.

On the trek to the Big Horn Mountains, August-September 1884, Roosevelt confided to Bill Merrifield that his grief was "beyond any healing." "Time... [will] never change me in that respect," he said. He declared again that he had "nothing to live for," and that little Alice "would be just as well off" being raised by the always-reliable Bamie.

Merrifield, who had recently buried his own wife, assured Roosevelt that time would heal his wounds. Roosevelt was inconsolable. "Now don't talk to me about time will make a difference—time will never change me in that respect."

Roosevelt's grief was genuine and when he confessed that he saw nothing left to live for, undoubtedly he meant it. But he was an enormously resilient man. During that same period he could write, "Black care rarely sits behind a rider whose pace is fast enough." It is clear that in throwing himself with all his mighty energy into the most difficult, time-consuming, fatiguing, and unglamorous duties of cowboy and ranch life, and riding along the badlands ridges at breakneck speed, Roosevelt was doing everything in his power to beat back "black care." It worked. By the time he left the badlands for a New York visit in 1885 he had essentially recovered. He did everything in his power for the rest of his life to dwell upon the death of Alice as little as possible, including avoiding conversations about her with his daughter Alice (who resented his reticence), and making no mention of his first wife in his 1913 *Autobiography*.

Within 21 months of Alice's death, Roosevelt was secretly engaged to his old childhood sweetheart Edith Carow. In fact, he had fallen in love so quickly that he felt considerable guilt and even self-loathing, and he worried that he was committing outrage to Victorian mourning protocols.

The badlands had done their magic.

What Were Roosevelt's Encounters with Indians During the Badlands Years?

On the Big Horn expedition in August and September 1884, Roosevelt and his two colleagues (Bill Merrifield and a muleteer named Norman Lebo) engaged in a target shooting contest with a group of friendly Cheyenne Indians near Crazy Woman Creek in northern Wyoming. The date was August 30, 1884. The contest was Merrifield's idea. He thought that by showing the Cheyenne individuals his and Roosevelt's marksmanship, they would lessen the chances that the Indians would attempt to interfere with the party's travels through northern Wyoming.

Roosevelt's principal Indian encounter occurred in 1885 somewhere northeast of the Elkhorn Ranch, probably in the vicinity of the northern Killdeer Mountains. Roosevelt was riding alone in what he called "debatable territory" on the margins of the Fort Berthold Indian Reservation. At that time, the reservation extended west all the way to today's Williston, and it intersected with the Little Missouri southeast of today's Watford City.

Suddenly five Indians (probably Hidatsa) "rode up over the further rim" of the plateau Roosevelt was crossing.

"The instant they saw me they whipped out their guns and raced full speed at me, yelling and flogging their horses," he wrote. "I at once leaped off him [Manitou] and stood with my rifle ready."

Roosevelt didn't wish to over-react, but he was a lone white man in the presence of five mounted Indians, in a countryside they knew much better than he did, not very long after the northern plains Indian wars that followed George Custer's reconnaissance of the Black Hills in 1874. Roosevelt was aware that a cowboy had recently been killed in this district, so he was unwilling to take any chances. In the *Autobiography* he wrote, "When I went West, the last great Indian wars had just come to an end, but there were still sporadic outbreaks here and there, and occasionally bands of marauding young braves were a menace to outlying and lonely settlements." Roosevelt did not want to become the victim of such a skirmish.

"I did not like their actions, and I thought it likely that if I allowed them to get hold of me they would at least take my horse and rifle, and possibly kill me."

Roosevelt dismounted and aimed his rifle at the closest Indian, just in case. "In a twinkling every man was lying over the side of his horse, and all five had turned and were galloping backwards, having altered their course as quickly as so many teal ducks."

One of the Indians made a peace sign. Roosevelt asked him what he wanted. Roosevelt reports him as saying, "How! Me good Injun, me good Injun." The man had a document indicating that he was a friendly, agency Indian, not a hostile. At the time, Indians were required to obtain passes from their agents to travel off of their reservations.

"I told him with sincerity that I was glad that he was a good Indian, but that he must not come any closer." The man asked Roosevelt for sugar and tobacco, neither of which Roosevelt was carrying in his saddle bags. "Another Indian began slowly drifting toward me in spite of my calling out to keep back, so I once more aimed with my rifle."

At this point, as Roosevelt reports the incident, "both Indians slipped to the side of their horses and galloped off, with oaths that did credit to at least one side of their acquaintance with English."

The Indians tailed Roosevelt for a couple of miles and then drifted away.

It is possible that Roosevelt over-reacted to what might have been only an appeal for food or the expectation of a token of payment for straying into country claimed by the Mandan, Hidatsa, and Arikara as their hunting grounds. It is also possible that Roosevelt correctly sensed danger and took rational steps to protect himself and his property. His behavior was unquestionably courageous, but it was also prudent and in some respects quite cautious. Roosevelt shared (and sometimes loudly proclaimed) many of the race prejudices of his time, but he would have been incapable of provoking an incident or initiating violence against any individual who had not directly threatened him.

The story seemed important enough to him to find its way into his *Autobiography* (1913), a book crowded with great national and international events. No doubt it validated his favorite maxim, "Speak softly but carry a big stick—you will go far."

Roosevelt tended to generalize in a Eurocentric, even at times bigoted, way about other cultures, but he was on the whole fair towards individuals. As a social Darwinist he found it hard to champion the cause of defeated nations, but once he got that sort of triumphalism out of his system, he was quite fair in his discussions of the winners and losers in the world's arena. He did not feel much sympathy for the Indian tribes that had been defeated by the United States Army, or cheated out of their land in the treaties of the Ninteenth Century. And yet he deplored the massacre at Wounded Knee (December 29, 1890), and he knew and respected individual Indians, a number of whom were members of his Rough Rider cavalry unit in 1898.

Is it True that Roosevelt Commissioned a Badlands Seamstress to Make Him a Buckskin Shirt?

Yes. Roosevelt met Gregor Lang and his son Lincoln in September 1883 at the mouth of Little Cannonball Creek, north of today's Marmarth, North Dakota. Nine months later, in June 1884, Roosevelt returned to the Lang's ranch to ask Lang senior to help draw up a contract increasing his investment in the badlands cattle industry.

On this second visit, Roosevelt asked Lincoln Lang, now 17 years old, to help him accomplish two goals. He wanted to kill an antelope and he wanted to obtain a genuine frontier buckskin shirt. Young Lang suggested that they ride east 25 miles to a ranch occupied by "Old Mrs. Maddox," a woman who might make Roosevelt the shirt he wanted, and meanwhile keep their eyes open for a pronghorn antelope on the rolling plains east of the badlands. Lang rightly understood that antelope prefer open country to the badlands.

Mrs. Maddox lived in the shadow of Black Butte on Sand Creek near today's Amidon, North Dakota. She was a colorful character, and Roosevelt clearly found much to appreciate in her besides her skill as a seamstress. In his *Autobiography*, he described her as "a very capable and very forceful woman, with sound ideas of justice and abundantly well able to hold her own." This was something of an understatement. Her husband got drunk and tried to beat her, but, as Roosevelt told the story, "She knocked him down with a stove-lid lifter, and the admiring bull whackers bore him off, leaving the lady in full possession of the ranch."

Roosevelt in shirt made by Mrs. Maddox in studio pose for *Hunting Trips of a Ranchman* (1885)

Given Mrs. Maddox's temper, one hopes Lang persuaded Roosevelt not to explain to her his theory of the buckskin shirt. "The fringed tunic or hunting shirt, made of buckskin," Roosevelt wrote, represented "the most picturesque and distinctly national dress ever worn in America. It was the dress in which Daniel Boone was clad when he first passed through the trackless forests of the Alleghenies... it was the dress worn by grim old Davy Crockett when he fell at the Alamo."

They arrived at the Maddox ranch just in time for dinner. According to Lang, Roosevelt and Mrs. Maddox hit it off. "Almost at once, she seemed to take a liking to Roosevelt, becoming quite chatty, which was unusual for her with strangers." "After dinner she measured him for his suit, promising it in a couple of weeks."

Roosevelt commissioned his Davy Crockett shirt and Mrs. Maddox got it to him on schedule, sometime later in 1884. In his *Autobiography* he explained that he used the shirt "for years, [and it] was used by one of my sons in Arizona a couple of winters ago" (almost thirty years later).

On the return ride that June day in 1884, Roosevelt managed to kill his first antelope, too. Lang said Roosevelt shouted "I got him! I got him!" He did his Indian war dance around the carcass, and impulsively offered his shotgun to Lang as a gift. Lang wrote, "Again and again he expressed satisfaction due both to my having been present to witness the occurrence and to my part in the undertaking. Nor was it mere empty talk. Before we left the scene he made that perfectly clear, handing me the surprise of my life in presenting me with a valuable shotgun which he had brought out from the east and which I knew was the only one he had."

Lang declined to accept the extravagant gift.

Roosevelt and Lang made the complete round trip of fifty miles on their horses in a single day, probably June 15, 1884, stopping frequently, Lang reported, to enable Roosevelt to study the flora and fauna, ask scores of questions, and exclaim about the beauties of the Dakota plains. One was 25, the other 17 years old.

Decades later Roosevelt remembered Mrs. Maddox and the shirt. Lincoln Lang remembered the young man who became the 26th President of the United States.

What Were the Names of Roosevelt's Horses?

We know the names of a few: Manitou, Sorrel Joe, Nell, Hackamore, Wire Fence, Pinto, Steel-Trap, War Cloud, Buckskin, Circus, and Standing Jimmie.

In his *Autobiography*, Roosevelt called Manitou "a wise old fellow, with nerves not to be shaken by anything." Manitou was Roosevelt's favorite. It was still alive in 1903 when Roosevelt, now President, made a brief stop at Medora on his way to Yellowstone National Park. His local friends were disappointed, even dismayed, when the President, heavily influenced by his secret service detail, declined to take a nocturnal ride on Manitou.

Manitou was clearly a special horse. "My own hunting-horse, Manitou, is the best and most valuable animal on the ranch. He is stoutly built and strong, able to carry a good-sized buck behind his rider for miles at a lope without minding it in the least; he is very enduring and very hardy, not only picking up a living but even growing fat when left to shift for himself under very hard conditions; and he is perfectly surefooted and as fast as any horse on the river. Though both willing and spirited, he is very gentle, with an easy mouth, and will stay grazing in one spot when left, and will permit himself to be caught without difficulty."

Roosevelt had ambivalent feelings about American Indians, but he liked Indian names. Manitou is a word from the Algonquian language group meaning "great spirit" or "god." During the badlands years he renamed the home he was building on Long Island "Sagamore," after Sagamore Mohannis, who Roosevelt believed had held councils on the site several centuries earlier. Sagamore is also an Algonquian word meaning "subordinate chief" or "war chief." The house had at first been called Leeholm, in honor of his first wife Alice Hathaway Lee.

Roosevelt had purchased a string of 52 ponies in the Black Hills in December 1884.

What Did Roosevelt Read in North Dakota?

Roosevelt was a voracious reader. He read a book a day most of his life. He made it a habit always to have a few books with him, even at times of hectic physical activity. At odd moments, he could be seen apart from the others quietly reading.

We have no complete list of the books he brought to Dakota. What we know about his reading habits during this period has to be assembled from scattered references.

In *Hunting Trips of a Ranchman*, Roosevelt mentioned a few of the titles he brought to Dakota Territory. "No ranchman who loves sport can afford to be without Van Dyke's *Still Hunter*, Dodge's *Plains of the Great West*, or Canton's *Deer and Antelope in America*; and Cone's *Birds of the Northwest* will be valued if he cares at all for natural history. As for Irving, Cooper, Hawthorne, Lowell and other standbys, I suppose no man whether East or West, would willingly be long without them. And for lighter reading there are Ike Marvel, Burrough's breezy pages, and the quaint, pathetic character sketches of the Southern writers, Cable, Craddock, Macon, Joel Chandler Harris and sweet Sherwood Bonner. And when one is in the Bad Lands, he feels as if they somehow look exactly like Poe's tales and poems sound."

In describing the Elkhorn Ranch in his *Autobiography*, Roosevelt wrote that he had "a bedroom for myself, and a sitting-room with a big fire-place. I got out a rocking chair—I am very fond of rocking chairs—and enough books to fill two or three shelves, and a rubber bathtub so that I could get a bath."

Roosevelt brought a copy of his best friend Henry Cabot Lodge's *Studies in Literature* to the West in 1884. It appears that he read it for the first time carefully on his Big Horn Mountains hunting trip, for he wrote a letter of thoughtful response and criticism to Lodge from the trail. "Did I tell you about my cowboys reading and in large part comprehending your 'Studies in Literature'? My foreman handed the book back to me to-day, after reading the 'Puritan Pepys' [chapter], remarking meditatively, and with, certainly, very great justice, that early Puritanism 'must have been darned rough on the kids.'"

It is intriguing to speculate about Roosevelt's access to the books of the Marquis and Marquise de Mores. They were avid readers, too, and with a more ambitious home in the badlands, they had a more extensive library than Roosevelt. We know from a letter Roosevelt wrote to his sister that he borrowed Tolstoy's *War and Peace* from Medora von Hoffman—probably in French. He seems to have gotten slightly fixated—not altogether positively—on Tolstoy during this period. We know he read both *War and Peace* and *Anna Karenina* in the Dakota badlands. Surely he was one of the first North Dakotans to read those two great works of Russian fiction.

The most famous reading incident in the badlands years involved Roosevelt's encounter with the three boat thieves in the spring of 1886. When it became necessary for Roosevelt to guard the thieves alone 24 hours per day, and march them overland from the Killdeer Mountains to the sheriff in Dickinson, he kept himself awake by reading the whole of Tolstoy's monumental *Anna Karenina*. Roosevelt greatly admired Tolstoy's breadth, his capacity to explore human situations without injecting judgments of any sort, and his narrative clarity, but he deplored the adultery of the protagonist Anna, and violently despised the novel's morally profligate character Stiva Oblonsky.

One would have thought the 900-page *Anna Karenina* was long enough to get Roosevelt through any ordeal, but he was a very fast reader and he had finished the novel before he got the ruffians to justice. So he asked the ringleader Red Headed Mike Finnegan if he happened to have any books with him. Finnegan had a dime novel about the exploits of Jesse James. Roosevelt promptly borrowed it to get himself through the adventure!

According to his own account, Roosevelt also read from the poetry of Matthew Arnold while he and his hired men were following the boat thieves down the Little Missouri River.

What Did Roosevelt Write in North Dakota?

Theodore Roosevelt was the writingest President in American history. Depending on how one counts, he wrote more than 30 books, compared to only a dozen by the second most prolific President, John Quincy Adams.

Several of Roosevelt's books are regarded as American classics: *The Naval War of 1812* (1882), *The Winning of the West* (four volumes, 1889-96), and the *Autobiography* (1913).

Roosevelt wrote portions of at least two books at his Elkhorn Ranch home on the Little Missouri River.

Roosevelt wrote some chapters of *Hunting Trips of a Ranchman* (published 1885) in Dakota Territory in the last weeks of 1884. Most of the manuscript (95,000 words), however, was written in New York between January 1 and March 8, 1885.

Hunting Trips was the first volume of a trilogy on his western experiences. The other two volumes, *Ranch Life and the Hunting Trail* (1888), and *The Wilderness Hunter* (1893), were published after Roosevelt had returned to New York. All contain stories and observations from the badlands years. *Ranch Life and the Hunting Trail* is of special interest because of the illustrations by Roosevelt's friend Frederic Remington. Roosevelt gave Remington photographs he had taken in Dakota Territory, which Remington used as the basis of his outstanding illustrations for the book.

Roosevelt's *Thomas Hart Benton* (1886) was a biography of the Missouri senator and ardent expansionist, produced for the American Statesmen series. His friend Henry Cabot Lodge, who was writing the life of Washington for the same series, had helped to win him the contract. Historians agree that *Benton* is a lively and intelligent, if somewhat superficial, biography, and that Roosevelt's portrait of Benton sounds a good deal like an autobiographical epitome of his own philosophy of the American West. Roosevelt wrote the first chapter at the end of March 1886, while his men built a makeshift boat with which Roosevelt subsequently hunted down the thieves who stole his good boat. On April 29, Roosevelt told his sister Bamie that he had written only one chapter, but by early June, he announced that he had written 85,000 words. All this in the Dakota badlands.

William Sewall described Roosevelt's writing habits. "Some days he would write all day long. Some days only part of the day.... Sometimes he would get so he could not write. Then he would take his gun and saunter off."

He wrote a few dozen extant letters during this period, some of which have been published in the eight-volume *Letters of Theodore Roosevelt*, edited by Elting E. Morrison. Roosevelt kept badlands diaries, but they are little more than spare notations about his whereabouts.

He also wrote a beautiful, if slightly over-the-top tribute to his first wife, Alice, in the badlands. *(see page 49)*.

How Close Did Roosevelt and the Marquis de Mores Come to Fighting a Duel?

Not very close. Roosevelt and de Mores were very similar in some ways, and fundamentally different in others. Both were aristocrats from elsewhere who came to the badlands in 1883, invested significant portions of their net wealth, and left after a few years of adventure and economic loss. They both took themselves very seriously, and they both were more likely to gravitate to trouble than turn away from it.

Roosevelt was much less wealthy than de Mores, but he lost a greater percentage of his net worth in Dakota than did the flamboyant Frenchman. He was also more modest in his idea of what profits the badlands of Dakota could be made to yield. Roosevelt sought to be a typical American cowboy and rancher. De Mores wanted to be the baron of the badlands. He built a slaughterhouse, purchased (or sponsored) most of the businesses in the village, which he founded and named after his wife Medora von Hoffman, and he entertained grandiose schemes to grow cabbages, transport fresh salmon from the west coast to Chicago and New York, and create a pottery industry on the banks of the Little Missouri.

By the time he reached Dakota Territory in 1883, de Mores had already killed two men in duels. He was a crack shot. He exercised his dueling arm by lifting a specially weighted walking stick until it was parallel with the ground. Roosevelt was an aggressive man, and he had knocked men down in the pubs of New York, but he had never been involved in a duel. His eyesight was poor. He was a more persistent and dogged than precise shot with a rifle; with a pistol he would be at a very decided disadvantage.

Roosevelt and de Mores maintained cordial although somewhat formal relations with each other. Roosevelt occasionally dined at the "chateau" de Mores, and the Marquis and Marquise dined with the Roosevelts in New York City during this period. On at least one occasion de Mores dined at the Elkhorn Ranch.

Still, they had found themselves in conflict a couple of times in the course of their badlands sojourns. De Mores had imperiously grazed cattle on Roosevelt's Maltese Cross acreage in the autumn of 1884, and removed them only when TR's ranch supervisors threatened to move the cattle themselves. Roosevelt chose for the location of the Elkhorn Ranch ground that de Mores claimed for himself. When de Mores protested, Roosevelt replied that all he found when he reconnoitered the site were carcasses of the Marquis' dead sheep, which he did not think would substantiate the Frenchman's claim in court. On another occasion, de Mores bought cattle from Roosevelt at an agreed-upon price, then unilaterally lowered the price when Roosevelt drove the cattle in to the slaughterhouse in Medora. When Roosevelt protested, de Mores said the price of cattle had dropped in eastern markets and he could not afford to pay Roosevelt more than the market value of the herd. Roosevelt took his cattle home, and determined to have no further business dealings with de Mores.

The so-called near-duel occurred in September, 1885. De Mores and his men had killed a man named Riley Luffsey in the spring of 1883, before Roosevelt ever set foot in the badlands. Although murder charges against de Mores had twice been dismissed for lack of evidence, in the fall of 1885 he was indicted for murder by a Mandan grand jury.

Roosevelt's friends and closest allies in the badlands were men who distrusted de Mores: especially Joe Ferris, Gregor Lang, and his son Lincoln. De Mores came to believe that Ferris had helped to round up witnesses against him at the time of the 1885 murder trial, and that Roosevelt was backing Ferris' activities. De Mores was misreading Ferris' actions (though not his attitude), and erroneously tying the murder indictment to what he regarded as increasing tensions with Roosevelt.

This led to a now-famous exchange of letters. From his jail cell in Mandan, de Mores wrote Roosevelt on September 3, 1885:

> My principle is to take the bull by the horns. Joe Ferris is very active against me and has been instrumental in getting me indicted by furnishing money to witnesses and hunting them up. The papers also publish very stupid accounts of our quarrelling—I sent you the paper to N.Y. Is this done by your orders? I thought you my friend. If you are my enemy I want to know it. I am always on hand as you know, and between gentlemen it is easy to settle matters of that sort directly.
>
> Yours very truly
> Mores
>
> I hear the people want to organize a county. I am opposed to it for one year more at least.

When he received this letter, Roosevelt regarded it as threatening a duel. He asked his ranch supervisor William Sewall to serve as his second, and his tentative choice of weapons was rifles at twelve paces. Roosevelt replied on September 6, 1885.

> Most emphatically I am not your enemy; if I were you would know it, for I would be an open one, and would not have asked you to my house nor gone to yours. As your final words, however, seem to imply a threat it is due to myself to say that the statement is not made through any fear of possible consequences to me; I too, as you know, am always on hand, and ever ready to hold myself accountable in any way for anything I have said or done.
>
> Yours very truly
> THEODORE ROOSEVELT

It seems clear in retrospect that de Mores was not threatening a duel, though he undoubtedly was putting Roosevelt on warning that he would not tolerate the New Yorker's meddling in his legal affairs. Roosevelt probably over-reacted to de Mores' letter, in part because he was never one to back away from a fight, and in part because he knew de Mores' penchant for settling disputes on the field of honor. After agonizing over the possibility of facing off against a man comfortable with violence, and of course an infinitely better marksman, Roosevelt decided that if a duel could not be avoided, he would choose rifles at twelve paces. Undoubtedly his logic was that rifles at such proximity would increase the likelihood that both men would be wounded or killed, and therefore

Marquis de Mores on horseback

de Mores might think twice before moving forward. Had he chosen pistols or swords, Roosevelt would have given de Mores a decided advantage.

At any rate, de Mores immediately sent a conciliatory letter to Roosevelt, which Roosevelt chose to interpret as an apology.

Is it True that Roosevelt and the Marquis de Mores Tried to Join a Band of Vigilantes?

Yes. Horse stealing had become endemic in western Dakota and eastern Montana Territories. A Montanan named Granville Stuart organized a band of vigilantes to rid the territory of desperadoes. Formal law had not yet come to the frontier. Lynch law was king.

Roosevelt and the Marquis de Mores were both men with a prickly sense of honor and a punctiliousness about property rights, and both had come west to seek adventures in one of America's last frontiers.

When they heard about the vigilante squad, they rode together to Miles City to meet Stuart. Their journey occurred sometime around June 26, 1884. They both thrilled to the idea of riding with vigilantes against ruffians on behalf of law and order. It was like a scene out of a dime novel.

They pleaded with Stuart to let them join the "stranglers," as the vigilantes were being called. Stuart refused on the grounds that both men were far too prominent for such grim—and anonymous—business.

Stuart was right. Roosevelt and de Mores had a penchant for getting their names in the nation's (and region's) newspapers. Both were publicity seekers. Neither could repress a good story, especially if they were the heroes of it. It is hard to imagine that Roosevelt could ever have become President of the United States if he had participated in a classical western lynching.

Picture this:

The Boat Thieves

Roosevelt owns an excellent boat, which he has tied up on the shore of the Little Missouri River outside the cabin at the Elkhorn Ranch. It is late March 1886. The initial spring thaw has come, but the river is choked with large blocks of ice.

He has just returned from the East and he is most eager to use the boat to go mountain lion hunting.

His ranch manager announces one morning that the boat is missing. The rope has been cut. A stray mitten is found on the shore.

Roosevelt concludes that someone has stolen his boat!

His men tell him that there is not much to do about it. The thieves have the boat. It would be difficult to follow them on the sodden shore, and getting through the ice floes to the river would be next to impossible. Besides, the thieves are long gone.

Roosevelt takes control. Lawlessness and theft can never be condoned, he explains, especially on the raw frontier where institutions of justice have not yet been established. Every unchallenged act of lawlessness invites further disregard for the sanctity of property. Every crime is a blow to the idea of civilization, especially where civilization is still fragile. The boat thieves must be apprehended, in spite of the miserable conditions on the river, the blizzard that is moving through the district, and the fact that the thieves have a boat and Roosevelt doesn't.

Roosevelt's men build a makeshift boat. It is not a handsome boat, but it floats. While they labor, Roosevelt takes advantage of his leisure time to write the first chapter of his forthcoming biography of Thomas Hart Benton.

At last the chase boat is ready. Roosevelt and his men load it with two weeks' provisions. The thieves have a six-day head start. Roosevelt is pretty sure he knows who they are. The ringleader is surely Red Headed Mike Finnegan, a notorious scofflaw and horse thief who is attempting to get out of the region before he is hanged for his offenses.

On the third day out, Roosevelt and his men catch up to the stolen boat. The thieves never expected to be followed in such weather. Two of them are off hunting. The third is a harmless old German named Pfaffenbach. Roosevelt and his cohorts arrest and disarm him, and then lay an ambush for the others. In the dramatic manner of a dime novel they manage to arrest the other two without violence, though Roosevelt will later report that "Finnigan hesitated for a second, his eyes fairly wolfish. Then, as I walked up within a few paces, covering the centre of his chest so as to avoid overshooting and repeating the command, he saw that he had no show, and, with an oath, let his rifle drop and held his hands up beside his head." Bully!

The boat has been recovered. The thieves are in Roosevelt's custody. Now all that remains is to get them to the authorities in Mandan. This can be done by floating everyone to the mouth of the Little Missouri River, then down the Missouri proper to Mandan, a distance of almost 200 river miles.

The desperadoes fulfill Roosevelt's fantasies about frontier adventure. Pfaffenbach is a harmless and empty-headed old man. Roosevelt will later make sure he is spared a jail term. Burnsted is what Roosevelt calls a sullen half-breed. And Finnegan was created for just such a lark as this. He has thick red hair, including facial hair, and evil black eyes. He cuts a mighty odd figure out there on the Little Missouri River because he is still recovering from a clever practical joke. One night he got drunk in the Medora bars and passed out cold. His friends borrowed a barber's shears and cut off all the hair on one side of his head, half of his beard, and half of his moustache on the same hemisphere. They even cut off all the fringe on one side of Finnegan's buckskin shirt. When he woke up he was a half-shorn man, and he was hopping mad. "His heart got bad," a contemporary said. "He laid down in a fringe of brush near the Marquis's store, where he could command a clear view of the town, and began to pump lead into every-thing in sight." By the time of the boat adventure, his hair is growing back, but he still bears the marks of the saloon joke.

Back on the river, Roosevelt is having trouble getting his boat thieves to justice.

It's so cold that Roosevelt dares not tie up the desperadoes at night, for fear that they will be frostbitten. So he and his two men mount a 24-hour watch. They force the thieves to remove their boots and socks at night so they will be less tempted to try to make a break for it.

It's almost impossible to make any progress. The river is choked with ice that repeatedly thaws and freezes again, and makes it difficult to move more than a mile or two downstream each day. The food supply is running out. The overflowing river makes shoreline hunting almost impossible. Eventually everyone is forced to eat unleavened bread made with muddy water scooped out of the Little Missouri.

Roosevelt considers turning the thieves loose as a humanitarian gesture. He cannot feed them and he cannot get them to jail. His old friend William Sewall convinces the boss to persevere. "It's something to know that if we're punishing ourselves, we're punishing the thieves also."

Fortunately, Roosevelt never travels without something to read. Better still, the book in his possession is a translation of Leo Tolstoy's interminable *Anna Karenina*. He reads it cover to cover to cut the tedium and to stay awake long enough to get the thieves to justice. He does not much like Tolstoy's indifference to morality—the novel is, after all, about adultery—but he admires the sweep of Tolstoy's imagination.

Eventually, Roosevelt decides he must abandon the idea of floating the thieves to Mandan. He'll march them overland to Dickinson instead, a distance of more than fifty miles. He scours the plains and finally reaches a remote cow camp, where he borrows a horse. Now he rides fifteen miles to the Diamond C Ranch on the southern edge of the Killdeer Mountains. There he obtains some desperately-needed supplies, and borrows a prairie wagon and a ranch hand to drive it. They go back for the thieves. Roosevelt leaves Sewall and Dow to take care of the boats. He will handle the three boat thieves alone.

So far the adventure is ten days old. The spring weather is just about as inhospitable as it could possibly be.

Roosevelt has finished *Anna Karenina*. In his guileless way he asks Red Headed Mike Finnegan if he might possibly have a book on his person. Finnegan does have a book! It's a dime novel about Jesse James. Roosevelt borrows it, and reads it through, too.

The adventure has become an ordeal. Alone with desperate men, Roosevelt knows that if he falls asleep even for an instant the thieves will abscond—or worse. Already profoundly fatigued and hungry, he now finds it necessary to stay awake for 48 straight hours.

For most of three days Roosevelt walks behind the wagon clutching his Winchester. He'd like to ride with the others, but he needs to keep his distance to avoid being overpowered by the ruffians, and he is not too sure about the virtue of the wagon driver either. The plains are sodden from the thaw, and Roosevelt finds it difficult to trudge through the ankle-deep gumbo and mud. At night they stay in a squalid hut. Roosevelt sits with his back to the door fighting off sleep, the Winchester nestled in his weary arms.

Finally the five men arrive in Dickinson. Roosevelt turns them in to the sheriff. For his efforts he receives $50—which includes mileage compensation for his 300-mile journey.

Roosevelt is triumphant. He has done the right thing in the face of almost impossible odds. It's his greatest adventure so far. But he's as tired as he has ever been, and his feet are bruised, swollen, and infected. He can barely walk.

He stops a man on the street and asks for directions to the nearest doctor. The stranger introduces himself as Dr. Victor Hugo Stickney, the only physician in the region. It's the Roosevelt luck.

Dr. Stickney takes Roosevelt to his office, and does what he can for the New Yorker's badly damaged feet. Stickney and Roosevelt, of course, become friends. Years later Stickney remembers how sorry Roosevelt looked as he trudged along the streets of Dickinson. "He was all teeth and eyes, but even so he seemed a man unusually wide awake. You could see he

Roosevelt's re-enactment of the boat thieves ordeal

was thrilled by the adventures he had been through. He did not seem to think he had done anything particularly commendable, but he was, in his own phrase, 'pleased as punch' at the idea of having participated in a real adventure." Roosevelt, said Stickney, "was just like a boy."

Roosevelt catches the next train west so he can get back to Medora in time for the spring meeting of the Little Missouri River Stockmen's Association, of which he is the president.

Roosevelt realizes that the story is so good that he must publish an account of it in *Century Magazine*. He writes a 4000-word narrative of his heroics. It would be such a better story if he had photographs to illustrate it. So he stages a couple of snapshots of the dramatic arrest of April 1, 1886, using Sewall and Dow as stand-ins for the desperadoes.

For the rest of his life, when he returns to North Dakota, Roosevelt reminds his audiences of his adventure with the boat thieves.

Did Edith Roosevelt Ever Visit the Badlands?

Yes. Roosevelt brought his second wife Edith, his sisters Anna (Bamie) and Corinne and her husband Douglas Robinson, a friend named Bob Ferguson, and his best friend Henry Cabot Lodge's sixteen-year-old son George (Bay) Lodge to the Elkhorn Ranch in 1890, not quite one year into North Dakota's statehood.

The group arrived on the train well before dawn on September 2, 1890. Met by Roosevelt's ranch supervisors Sylvane Ferris and Bill Merrifield, the party repaired to Joe Ferris' store to rest before making the long journey to the ranch, 35 miles north of Medora.

Edith's first impressions of North Dakota were not favorable. A rainstorm that Corinne called "one of the most frightful storms" she ever witnessed, soaked the traveling party as they exited the train and Edith's dress was covered with a "glutinous slime" before she even set foot in the depot. At first the stark badlands country struck her as godforsaken.

After a short rest, the men rode horses to the Elkhorn Ranch, while the ladies rode in a horse-drawn wagon. The party crossed the Little Missouri River 23 times before they reached the ranch. According to Corinne, the wagon had to hurtle down one steep bank of the river in order to gain enough momentum to climb the bank on the other side. Corinne said nobody dared complain lest they disappoint Theodore.

The Roosevelts reached the eight-room, 30- by 60-foot cabin at noon on September 2, 1890.

Edith cheered up, climbed a butte, chased prairie dogs, and rode a horse called Wire Fence. She laughed as Theodore's sister Corinne attempted to "wrastle" a calf.

Later, Roosevelt wrote gleefully to Edith's mother: "I have rarely seen Edith enjoy anything more than she did the six days at my ranch... and she looks just as well and pretty and happy as she did four years ago when I married her—indeed I sometimes almost think she looks if possible even sweeter and prettier, and she is as healthy as possible, and so young looking and slender."

The Roosevelt party was not in North Dakota long. After a week, on September 9, 1890, they boarded the train again and ventured on to Yellowstone Park. At Yellowstone Edith was thrown from her horse and badly bruised. Roosevelt briefly worried that she might have broken her back. But Edith was made of some of the same stuff as her hyperactive husband.

The party returned to Medora briefly on September 23, 1890, on its return trip to Washington, D.C.

This was Edith's only trip to the North Dakota badlands. It came at the end of Roosevelt's main period of badlands experiences, and in a sense, served to close the curtain on that episode of his life.

The Roosevelt family at Sagamore Hill

What Role Did Roosevelt Play in Creating a Stockmen's Association?

Several attempts had been made to organize the cattlemen of the Little Missouri River Valley before Roosevelt got involved. Howard Eaton had done some preliminary work to get ranchers interested in an association and had called for meetings on a couple of occasions, without success.

Then Theodore Roosevelt, a born leader and lover of organizations, took up residence in Dakota Territory in 1884.

The need for a stockmen's association was acknowledged by almost everyone in the badlands. Horse thieves were working eastern Montana and western Dakota Territories virtually unmolested. Because there were few fences and herds from up and down the valley intermingled, close cooperation was essential during the twice-annual roundup to sort out and return everyone's stray cattle. The casual system of siting ranches and defining grazing rights inevitably led to conflict. Some agreement about what constituted over-grazing needed to be reached—and then enforced. Billings County was not formally organized until 1886. The nearest United States Marshall was 200 miles south at Deadwood. The nearest magistrate was in Dickinson, 35 miles east. The nearest sheriff was in Mandan, 140 miles away.

Roosevelt called a meeting of interested ranchers for December 19, 1884. Between November 16, when he arrived at Medora, and the date of the meeting, Roosevelt rode up and down the Little Missouri River Valley talking with ranchers and urging them to participate in the organization.

The organizational meeting on December 19 has become the stuff of Roosevelt and badlands legends. About a dozen ranchers (or their representatives) attended, and a number of others sent letters endorsing the goals of the proposed organization. Roosevelt was elected chairman of the meeting, even though he was not one of the principal stockmen, not very experienced in ranch life, and clearly a temporary and occasional resident of the Little Missouri River Valley.

Some sort of confrontation occurred at the meeting, which was held at Roberts Hall in Medora. Fred A. Willard, a violent and abusive man who was also the Deputy United States Marshall for the district, attempted to intimidate Roosevelt. At the very least, sharp words were exchanged before Willard withdrew. According to one lurid account, Willard actually drew his pistol and held it against Roosevelt's stomach, and Roosevelt shouted, "Shoot and be damned....you pledged your honor to uphold the laws of the United States and you are in league with the lawbreakers....Get out!" Other eyewitnesses dispute the idea that guns were drawn, but acknowledge that Roosevelt refused to be bullied, and succeeded in pushing Willard out the door. Years later, perhaps embellishing the story for effect, Roosevelt said, "There was no other way, and it had exactly the effect we desired. I do not think I was in any danger. I was unarmed, and if he had shot me down he knew he could not have escaped swift retribution. Besides, I was right, and he knew it!"

At any rate, the meeting accomplished its goals. Seven resolutions were passed, one of which empowered Roosevelt to write up bylaws for the stockmen's association. The Marquis de Mores was appointed as a committee of one to work with the eastern

Montana grazing association to encourage the territorial legislature to pass laws favorable to the cattle industry. The organization was to be called the Little Missouri River Stockmen's Association. Roosevelt kept the minutes of the meeting in his own handwriting.

Thereafter the association met twice annually. It sent delegations, including Roosevelt, to the Montana Stockgrowers Association meetings in Miles City during those boom years, and did what it could to bring order to the cattle business and prevent the spread of communicable diseases. Then came the winter of 1886-87, which shattered the complacency of everyone on the northern plains.

The meeting on April 16, 1887, was a somber one. According to the *Dickinson Press*, "The Little Missouri Stockmen's Association met at Medora on Saturday of last week with a slim attendance. The meeting adjourned without transacting much business of importance. Owing to the heavy losses during the past winter it was not thought worth while to appoint a general round up for the spring...."

Clearly there would have been a grazing association in the Dakota badlands if Roosevelt had never ventured west from New York City. His role was to get the association organized sooner rather than later, to keep it focused on its mission and tasks, and to preside over the meetings with his usual firmness and commitment to parliamentary procedure.

De Mores roundup, Medora, ca. 1880-1885

Everyone joins in singing, "America." Dinner is served. America, if it stands for anything, stands for abundance.

Once everyone has had a chance to regroup, the first orator, John Rea, speaks patriotic bombast: "the United States, bounded on the north by the Aurora Borealis, on the south by the precession of the equinoxes, on the east by primeval chaos, and on the west by the Day of Judgment." In Roosevelt's eyes, mere boilerplate.

Now young Roosevelt, vouched for by Dr. Stickney himself, rises to speak. A witness says he is "plainly embarrassed," and that his voice was so high that it was reckoned "between a squeak and a shriek."

Twice he identifies himself with the men and women who have gathered to celebrate American freedom. "We grangers and cowboys alike," he squeaks, "have opened a new land." Later, in a more somber spirit, he says, "I am, myself, at heart as much a Westerner as an Easterner; I am proud, indeed, to be considered one of yourselves."

Is this true? Do the permanent citizens of northern Dakota Territory, gathered in Dickinson, consider the gesticulating New Yorker one of themselves?

Roosevelt's theme is not "the gifts and blessings of America," but rather duty. He says pleasant words about the *Declaration of Independence*, but he does not tell his audience that he actually despises Thomas Jefferson, whom he considers the weakest executive in American history, with the possible exception of his lackey James Madison. This is not the time for that discussion.

He reminds the pioneers of Dickinson that they will have deep influence on the course of Dakota history, because they represent the head of a stream that will flow onward through the course of time: "our efforts have infinitely more effect, in bending it in any given direction, than they would have if they were made farther along." There is a stiff and growing wind in Dickinson—it is possible that Roosevelt's riparian metaphor is lost on the crowd.

He makes one of his first assaults on what he will later call "hyphenated Americans." "We welcome every honest immigrant," he says, "no matter from what country he comes, provided only that he leaves off his former nationality."

He flatters the people by telling them that here in America they "are sovereigns, not subjects," but then he reminds them that—as sovereigns—they have the grave responsibility of governing themselves with wisdom and integrity. Roosevelt admits that he is addressing the folks in a "rather solemn strain to-day, because of my pride in you, and because your welfare, moral as well as material, is so near my heart."

Wait. Wasn't he just saying he likes to think of himself as one of them? Now he is telling them he is proud of them? Which is it, Mr. Roosevelt?

Then he lets it rip and gives them the essence of his being: "Like all Americans, I like big things; big prairies, big forests and mountains, big wheat fields, railroads,—and herds of cattle, too—big factories, steamboats, and everything else. But we must keep steadily in mind that no people were ever yet benefited by riches if their prosperity corrupted their virtue."

Imagine, as backdrop for this moment in Roosevelt's life, one of those old end-of-broadcast-day television segments, or Encyclopedia Britannica films, with the flag billowing majestically and aerial b-roll of giant wheat fields stretching to the horizon, purple mountains in majesty, the Mississippi and Missouri Rivers gathering the heartland's waters, a steam locomotive drawing a hundred gleaming cars into a mountain tunnel or trestling over the gorge, a lone Indian on horseback looking on wistfully.

Isn't it clear? Theodore Roosevelt is ready for the big time.

Afterwards, Roosevelt and editor Packard return to Medora, this time in a passenger car. Roosevelt cannot get his theme of responsible citizenship, good government, and the necessity that American society match the magnificence of the scenery out of his mind.

Finally, Packard predicts that his companion will become the President of the United States. Roosevelt "was not in the least surprised by my statement," Packard later remembered. "He gave me the impression of having thoroughly considered the matter and to have arrived at the same conclusion."

Says Roosevelt: "If your prophecy comes true, I will do my part to make a good one."

Which of course he does.

Pages 86-87:
Roosevelt addressing North Dakotans at Fargo in 1903

What Was Roosevelt's Relationship with A.T. Packard?

Arthur Packard was the editor of the *Bad Lands Cow Boy*, which he published between February 1884 and January 1887, "not... for fun, but for $2 per year." Packard was a thoughtful, articulate, sometimes sardonic graduate of the University of Michigan, enjoying a temporary sojourn on the Dakota frontier. He was just the sort of man Roosevelt admired. Roosevelt called him "a good fellow, a college graduate, and a first-class baseball player."

Roosevelt and Packard apparently met in Bismarck in late September 1883. Packard was then the editor of the *Bismarck Tribune*. Roosevelt had stopped on his way back east to get his buffalo head stuffed.

Packard established the *Bad Lands Cow Boy* in February 1884. Roosevelt returned to Medora in June 1884 after the simultaneous deaths of his wife and mother on Valentine's Day and severe political setbacks at the Republican national convention in early June. "He liked chatting with the men who liked the smell of printers' ink," Packard wrote years later. Because Roosevelt craved gatherings of talkative men, but did not frequent saloons, the office of the *Bad Lands Cow Boy* became a refuge where he could hear the latest news from the badlands and beyond, and make pronouncements to a highly intelligent, if somewhat skeptical, young newspaperman.

Packard advised Roosevelt not to carry a handgun in the village of Medora. He suggested that Roosevelt deposit his gun in Packard's office whenever he came to town. His view was that handguns invite more trouble than they forestall, and that real gunmen were so much better with pistols that it would be suicide to stand up to them. To prove his point to Roosevelt, Packard set up a demonstration. A local gunman, William Roberts, put ten bullets into two tomato cans that Packard and Roosevelt threw simultaneously into the air. Roosevelt was deeply impressed. "A revolver is a mere foolish encumbrance for any but a trained expert and need never be carried," Roosevelt subsequently wrote.

On the whole, Packard regarded Roosevelt as a better civil leader than a genuine cowboy. His frequent accounts of Roosevelt's activities and comings and goings have a wry quality to them. Roosevelt's first appearance in the *Bad Lands Cow Boy* set the tone. "Theodore Roosevelt," wrote Packard, "the young New York reformer, made us a very pleasant call Monday, in full cowboy regalia." Packard would never have said that about a real cowboy.

Packard was a believer in law and order. As justice of the peace in Medora, he carried a printer's rule rather than a sidearm, and, like Roosevelt, he was fearless in the face of lawlessness and disorder.

On July 4, 1886, Packard became one of the first Americans to predict that Theodore Roosevelt would become the President of the United States.

Why Did Roosevelt Get Out of the Cattle Business?

Roosevelt left Dakota Territory for several reasons. He had considered making his living from ranching and writing in the wake of a series of setbacks in 1884. First, his wife Alice and mother Mittie died within hours of each other on February 14, 1884, in Roosevelt's New York City brownstone. In the depths of his grief, Roosevelt wrote, "For joy or for sorrow my life has now been lived out."

Roosevelt had also suffered a significant political setback in 1884. The reform wing of the Republican Party had tried desperately to prevent the nomination of James Blaine of Maine as the party's Presidential candidate. Roosevelt and his friend (soon to be his closest friend) Henry Cabot Lodge worked hard to promote the candidacy of George F. Edmunds of Vermont. When Blaine was nominated, many of the Republican Party's severest reformists (called Mugwumps) bolted and determined to support the Democrat Grover Cleveland in the November election. In the end, Roosevelt and Lodge decided to hold their noses and support the Republican ticket. This brought denunciations from the progressive wing of the party and from many newspaper editorialists.

In June 1884, Roosevelt had good reason to think his political career might be over.

As time began to heal these wounds between June 1884 and the fall of 1886, Roosevelt's motive for burying himself in the badlands receded. It was clear by the end of 1885 that he would be welcomed back into New York politics, and in 1886 he was recruited to represent the Republican Party in the mayoral election in New York City.

Perhaps more to the point, Roosevelt fell in love in 1885 with an easterner, his childhood sweetheart Edith Carow. He had not expected to remarry at all, certainly not so soon. Victorian sensibilities mandated a prolonged mourning period. Roosevelt was embarrassed to acknowledge that he had fallen in love less than two years after the death of Alice. Marriage to Edith essentially ruled out a prolonged life in the Dakota badlands. The badlands years were the adventure of a single man. Marriage and family would draw him back to New York.

Although he declared in Dickinson on July 4, 1886, that "I am, myself, at heart, as much a Westerner as an Easterner," the fact is that Roosevelt was all of his life an easterner who spent some of his discretionary time in the West, rather than the other way around.

The disastrous winter of 1886-87 not only shattered any notion that Roosevelt was going to profit from the cattle business, but it damaged Roosevelt's romance with the Dakota badlands. He was on his honeymoon in Europe when he learned of the devastating losses that he and every other rancher had sustained. As soon as he returned from his European honeymoon, Roosevelt made a trip to the badlands to inspect the damage. To Lodge, he wrote, "The losses are crippling. For the first time I have been utterly unable to enjoy a visit to any ranch. I shall be glad to get home."

Finally, Roosevelt had, by late 1886, accomplished what he had really intended. He had thrown himself unhesitatingly into the frontier life, overcome fears and inhibitions, bonded with average Americans and learned to respect them deeply, transformed both his body and his spirit, participated in what he took to be the quintessential American experience, and had a roaring good time in chaps and sombrero. His soul was too large to confine itself to just one experience or one arena, however satisfying. He had taken a transfusion from the Little Missouri River Valley that would serve him for the rest of his life.

But he was ready to return to the East.

How Much Money Did Roosevelt Lose in the Cattle Business?

Approximately $23,500. His investment in the Maltese Cross and Elkhorn ranches was approximately $82,500. His losses came mostly in the disastrous winter of 1886-87 when ranchers across the northern plains lost 60-75% of their herds. Before that winter Roosevelt's herds were increasing in size, and he was realizing modest profits from his ranch operations.

Before he ventured into the Dakota badlands, Roosevelt was a moderately wealthy man. From his father he inherited $125,000. When his mother Mittie died in 1884, he inherited an additional $62,500.

He had managed (barely) to live within his income before he began to invest in Dakota ranches in a serious way.

His initial outlay was $14,000 in September 1883. In the early summer of 1884, Roosevelt invested another $26,000. In December 1884 TR bought 52 horses at a cost of $3,275. In May 1885, he purchased 1500 additional cows at a cost of $39,000. Eventually, he owned somewhere between 3500 and 5000 head of cattle on his two ranches.

After the ruinous winter of 1886-87, Roosevelt made a visit to the badlands to survey his losses. "I am bluer than indigo about the cattle," he wrote his sister. "It is even worse than I feared; I wish I was sure I would lose not more than half the money ($80,000) I invested out here. I am planning to get out."

Roosevelt's accounts were not very detailed, so it impossible to determine just how much he invested altogether. Nor did he provide complete details of his losses.

Roosevelt did not entirely abandon the cattle business after 1887, however. He downsized, reorganized, and kept up ranch operations until 1898, when he sold what was left of his herd to his old friend Joe Ferris. Roosevelt was not finally out of the cattle business altogether until he assumed the Presidency in 1901.

Roosevelt's ledgers indicate a net loss of $23,556.68 on his badlands investments. That doesn't count the amount of interest he would have received for his 80,000-plus dollars had he merely left his inheritance in savings accounts.

When Was the Last Time Roosevelt Visited North Dakota?

October 6, 1918, just three months before his death. Roosevelt stopped in Bismarck and Fargo that day on a national speaking tour during the last days of World War I. His theme was "uncompromising Americanism" at a time when the government of North Dakota was controlled by farmer-socialists of the war-critical Nonpartisan League. Two-thousand people gathered to glimpse the former President that Sunday morning in Bismarck. Roosevelt had not intended to speak, but NPL signs among the crowd provoked him to address them for a short time. He recalled his arrest of the boat thieves in 1886, said, "I owe more to the times when I lived out here and worked with the men who have been my friends than to anything else," and urged the mothers of North Dakota to scorn peace talk until American troops "whip Germany to her knees."

His remarks in Fargo were very brief. He called for the unconditional surrender of Germany, and warned Dakotans not to be taken in by the current German peace offensive.

He did not, on that trip, visit Medora.

The last time he visited the badlands was in April, 1911. He was beginning his run for a third term as President. His brief stop in Medora was unremarkable, but a previous stop in Beach led to local disenchantment. After expressing his surprise that Beach existed at all, Roosevelt warned the local ranchers that they should attempt to put no more than one cow on every twelve acres of such marginal grassland. For these words of caution, the once-revered Roosevelt was taunted by local citizens. One declared that Roosevelt was an anachronism, preferring nostalgia for a distant past to the grazing potential of the new century.

Roosevelt's last sustained visit to the Little Missouri River Valley came in 1896. He hunted at the Elkhorn Ranch. It turned out to be his last visit to the ranch.

When a badlands visit was proposed in 1918 Roosevelt said, "It's a mistake for one to hit the back trail after many years have passed. One finds things changed, the old picture destroyed, the romance gone.... It's best that it should be so, but I don't wish to see the place again. I'd rather try and remember it as it was."

The romance was over.

Did Any of the Rough Riders Come from North Dakota?

In 1898 Roosevelt assembled what he called a troupe of "harum-scarum roughriders" to fight in Cuba in the Spanish-American War. Technically the regiment was called the First Volunteer Cavalry, but it was soon known as "Teddy's Terrors," "Teddy's Cowboy Contingent," and eventually "Roosevelt's Rough Riders." There were 23,000 applications from all over America for fewer than 800 positions. Just over 600 of the volunteers went to Cuba.

Roosevelt described the men "as typical an American regiment as ever marched or fought. I suppose about 95 per cent of the men are of native birth, but we have a few from everywhere, including a score of Indians and about as many men of Mexican origin from New Mexico; then there are some fifty Easterners—almost all graduates of Harvard, Yale, Princeton, etc.—and almost as many Southerners; the rest are men of the plains and the Rocky Mountains. Three fourths of our men have at one time or another been cowboys or else are small stockmen; certainly two thirds have fathers who fought on one side or the other in the civil war."

So far as we know, only two of the Rough Riders had known Roosevelt in Dakota Territory. One was Fred Herrig. He was not one of the "permanent" residents of Dakota Territory, but he had apparently done some hunting with Roosevelt in the 1880s. In *The Rough Riders*, Roosevelt wrote, "A dozen years before he and I had hunted mountain sheep and deer when laying in the winter stock of meat for my ranch on the Little Missouri, sometimes in the bright fall weather, sometimes in the Arctic bitterness of the early Northern winter." Roosevelt wrote that Herrig spoke English with a thick Alsatian accent and that he was an excellent trailsman.

The other was Jesse Langdon, who met Roosevelt in the badlands a decade previously, when his father W.C. Langdon, a veterinarian, had visited Dakota ranches to inspect cattle for Texas fever. Jesse had been seven years old back then. He later recalled that, in his childhood, he had been frightened by Roosevelt's thick glasses. Now 17, in San Antonio, he declared, "I'm Jesse Langdon. I've hoboed by train all the way from North Dakota and I want to join your Rough Riders." "Can you ride a horse?" Roosevelt asked. "I can ride anything that's got hair on it," Langdon said. "Then go upstairs and tell them I sent you."

There were two other North Dakotans among the voluntary cavalry unit: William T. Zychlinski of Bismarck, and Frank Kania of Jamestown.

Roosevelt's "crowded hour," what he later described as the "great day of my life," was the Rough Riders' assault on Kettle Hill near Santiago, Cuba, on July 1, 1898.

What Was Roosevelt's Larger Impact on North Dakota?

The badlands Roosevelt visited in September 1883 were still part of Dakota Territory, which had been created in 1861.

Statehood came on November 2, 1889. As statehood approached, there was speculation that Roosevelt would become one of the first Senators from North Dakota. By then Roosevelt's sojourn in the Little Missouri River Valley was drawing to an end and he was re-entering political life in New York. After he became engaged to his second wife, Edith Carow, in 1885, Roosevelt ceased to declare that he was thinking of making Dakota his permanent home.

Even so, he never forgot North Dakota, and he made sure the 39th state received the benefits of Presidential patronage.

As President, Roosevelt doubled the number of National Parks from five to ten. He added Crater Lake in Oregon (1902), Wind Cave in South Dakota (1903), Mesa Verde in Colorado (1906), Platt in Oklahoma (1906), and Sullys Hill in North Dakota (1904) to the National Park system. Platt and Sullys Hill have since been demoted (1976; 1931). Sullys Hill, at Devils Lake, is now a National Game Preserve.

If Roosevelt increased the size and sanctity of the National Parks, he actually invented the National Wildlife Refuge System! Concerned that hunters were destroying egrets and pelicans on an island in the Indian River in Florida, Roosevelt asked his Attorney General Philander Knox if any law permitted him to designate federal bird sanctuaries. Knox said no such law existed. President Roosevelt then asked if any law *prevented* him from creating bird sanctuaries. Knox said no. "Very well, then I so declare it," Roosevelt cried, and on that date, March 14, 1903, what would become the National Wildlife Refuge System was born. Roosevelt designated 51 federal bird sanctuaries during his Presidential tenure, including two in North Dakota. Chase Lake in Stutsman County was designated on August 28, 1908, and Stump Lake in Nelson County was added to the system on March 9, 1905. Today North Dakota has 63 National Wildlife Refuges, more than any other state.

On June 17, 1902, Roosevelt signed the Newlands Reclamation Act, creating a new federal bureau whose mission was to reclaim arid western lands through government-funded irrigation systems. The first 24 federal irrigation projects were authorized during the Roosevelt administration, including the Lower Yellowstone Project on May 10, 1904. Although the Yellowstone River makes most of its run in Montana, the last 17 miles are in northwestern North Dakota. The Lower Yellowstone irrigation system is still functioning at the beginning of the Twenty-first Century.

In a larger, but less direct, sense, the Little Missouri National Grasslands are a legacy of Roosevelt's concept of federal supervision of the public domain. The National Grasslands were formally created in 1960, but they had existed as Land Utilization Projects since 1934. In his Seventh Annual Message to Congress, December 3, 1907, Roosevelt wrote, "There must be a realization of the fact that to waste, to destroy, our natural resources, to skin and exhaust the land instead of using it so as to increase its usefulness, will result in undermining until the days of our children the very prosperity which we ought by right to hand down to them amplified and developed." Roosevelt did not live to see the creation of the National Grasslands, but he would undoubtedly have approved of the combination of federal supervision and local grazing association self-management of his beloved badlands.

Perhaps most significant of all, Roosevelt provided North Dakota one of the most colorful chapters of its frontier heritage. North Dakota is regarded by most outsiders as a cold, isolated, and not very interesting place, flat farmland at the northern boundary of the nation. Roosevelt's adventures in Dakota Territory provide a tincture of romance and grandeur that people everywhere can appreciate.

North Dakota has one claim that no other state can make. It was the second home of Theodore Roosevelt. In some respects it was a more important home than his estate on Long Island, for it was here, in Dakota, that Roosevelt was transformed into the man we associate with his national legend.

A great man lived among us. A future President of the United States. The spirit of the place got under his skin. In fact, it transformed him forever. He was not afraid to say it played a significant role in his later achievements. In subtle ways, Roosevelt changed the destiny of North Dakota and the characters of some, at least, of its inhabitants.

Did Roosevelt Mean it When He Said He Would Never Have Been President Were it Not for His Experiences in North Dakota?

Yes. But he may not have been right about that. He was a man of enormous political talent, coupled with a deep, even profound political ambition. He had very definite ideas about the course the United States needed to take as it entered the Twentieth Century. His energies were cyclonic. It is hard to think that he could have been kept out of the Presidency by anything short of a scandal or early death. "You are rushing so rapidly to the front," wrote his closest friend Henry Cabot Lodge on August 31, 1895, "that the day is not far distant when you will come into a large kingdom."

There is no doubt, however, that Roosevelt realized that he had undergone a transformation in the American West, and the location of that drama was the badlands of Dakota Territory. It was a double transformation: in Dakota he turned the corner on his physical frailty and emerged as a man wholly capable of, as well as deeply committed to, the strenuous life. Perhaps more important, Roosevelt learned an essential lesson of democracy in the Dakota badlands. He learned to respect and love average Americans of the heartland, and to understand that they were not fundamentally different from himself, or he from them. Roosevelt's democratic idealism and his essential populism, his ability to identify himself with common men and women doing unheralded things, served him all of his adult life and gave him an enormous advantage over his political competitors.

In a sense, what Roosevelt meant by his statement of 1910 was that the American West, specifically the Dakota badlands, taught him how to connect with all the people of the United States, and thereby to distinguish himself from scores of other well-meaning but more or less disconnected politicians who sought high office.

In North Dakota Roosevelt learned a great deal about what he called "the glory of work and the joy of living."

Put it another way. A great leader has to be tested. Roosevelt's life from 1858 until 1883 had sometimes been difficult, but he was a privileged young man with a strong mind who had done pretty well so far, with the aid of an appreciative and helpful social establishment in New York and Boston. Before 1883 there was nothing very remarkable about his life. By deciding to master cowboy and ranch life, and to test himself in the arena where he was least gifted, Roosevelt discovered gumption and stamina and resilience in himself that he might not have known he possessed if he had remained in the comfortable world of eastern social clubs and political circles. It is doubtful that he ever worked as hard, stayed awake so long at a stretch, pushed his body to such limits, or endured such harsh weather, as he did between 1883 and 1887 in Dakota.

Another way of understanding the famous declaration is that Roosevelt was saying he would never have become *the kind of President* he was had it not been for that testing time on the northern plains. He was certainly the most strenuous President in American history. He had begun to seek the strenuous life long before he shot his first buffalo, but that period deepened what became a lifelong quest, and set it in concrete.

At any rate, it would be a mistake to conclude that Roosevelt made that famous utterance primarily to flatter the people of North Dakota. It seems clear that Roosevelt gained more from us than we have ever gained from him.

How Did the Cabin from the Maltese Cross Ranch Wind Up in Medora?

By a long and circuitous route. The cabin was built for Roosevelt by Sylvane Ferris and Bill Merrifield between September 1883 and June 1884. Roosevelt occupied it off and on during his badlands years, though he preferred to spend his time at the more spacious house at the more remote Elkhorn Ranch once it was ready in the spring of 1885.

At the end of Roosevelt's badlands years, the Maltese cabin was sold. In 1903, while Roosevelt was serving as the 26th President of the United States, the state of North Dakota purchased the cabin from its owner, a man named Jack Snyder.

After it was photographed from all angles, and after each log was numbered with chalk inside and out, the cabin was dismantled for the 1200 mile journey to St. Louis, where it was exhibited at the 1904 World's Fair and Louisiana Purchase Exposition. It was the centerpiece of the North Dakota Agricultural Display.

The Chimney Butte cabin was just one of several Presidential log houses at the World's Fair. Lincoln's boyhood cabin from Kentucky was there,

Roosevelt's Maltese Cross cabin minus its original roof

as well as one associated with Ulysses S. Grant.

Historians have asserted that more than a million people visited the Roosevelt cabin in St. Louis. One of the visitors was President Roosevelt himself—in September 1904. Roosevelt had a slightly difficult time identifying the cabin out of its badlands context, in part because the roof had been altered by occupants after his period in Dakota Territory. "If Sylvane Ferris said it's the cabin, then it must be it," declared the President of the United States.

One year later, the cabin was moved 2000 miles west to Portland, Oregon, for the Lewis and Clark Exposition marking the centennial of America's most famous voyage of discovery. The Roosevelt cabin was displayed for 137 days in the North Dakota exhibit in the Palace of Agriculture. A quarter of a million people saw it there.

Plans to move the cabin permanently to Roosevelt's home at Oyster Bay, Long Island, did not materialize.

After the 1904-05 national tour, the cabin spent two years on the North Dakota State Fair Grounds at Fargo, where it was on loan to an orphanage, the Children's Home Society of Fargo.

In 1908 the cabin found its way to the capitol grounds in Bismarck, North Dakota, where it would remain for the next fifty years. For the first eleven years it was neglected. Souvenir hunters defaced the structure, which had deteriorated severely thanks to its extensive travels, repeated dismantling and reconstruction, the press of visitors at St. Louis and Portland, and the severities of North Dakota weather. In 1919 the *Bismarck Tribune* wrote, "Crumbling away to dust on the North Dakota Capitol Grounds is the Roosevelt Cabin, one of America's shrines."

At that point the Minishoshe Chapter of the Daughters of the American Revolution (DAR) took control. They petitioned the State Board of

Administration to permit them to assume responsibility for the cabin. The DAR raised funds for the stabilization and partial restoration of the building. By 1923 the cabin was ready to receive visitors again.

Finally, in 1959, just after the centennial of Roosevelt's birth, the cabin was moved to the grounds of Theodore Roosevelt National Park (south unit) in Medora, North Dakota. It has been there ever since. Under the supervision of the National Park Service, the cabin was restored as much as possible to its original condition. It was in Medora, for example, that the original pitched roof was restored.

What Were Roosevelt's Relations with Medora von Hoffman?

Roosevelt apparently met Medora von Hoffman de Mores for the first time in the badlands of Dakota Territory. There is no evidence that he knew her in New York City prior to his adventures in the badlands.

Though she has been somewhat obscured by virtue of having lived in the shadow of her flamboyant husband, Medora von Hoffman was an extraordinary woman in her own right. Daughter of a German-born New York banker, with an immense annual allowance, she met the Marquis in Paris. They were married on February 15, 1882, at La Verriere in southern France.

She brought twenty servants with her to the badlands of Dakota. Although she was not as overbearing as her husband, she was capable of being rude to the men and women of the frontier, even when she was accepting their hospitality. In her 26-room "chateau," which looked down upon the de Mores' empire, she entertained her family

Medora von Hoffman

and visiting aristocrats, but the common people of the valley were not often made welcome.

She was the sort of woman Roosevelt found irresistible: womanly, adventuresome, brainy, fiercely dedicated to family life. She was a serious student of world history. She spoke seven languages. She played the piano and she was a painter of some talent. Several of her watercolors of the Little Missouri River Valley survive. The cover of this guidebook reproduces one of her badlands watercolors.

One of Medora's passions was hunting. She must have cut a remarkable figure in her hunting trousers, black sombrero with an eagle feather, riding sidesaddle over the breaks country of Dakota and Montana Territories. She was apparently a crack shot, according to witnesses, better even than her husband.

The *Daily Pioneer Press* could not resist wry comment: "This is as it should be, and shows what a woman of spirit can do in this glorious Western country. It will not be long, at this rate, before the marquise will be running the cold storage business singlehanded and the marquis will be relegated to look after the minor details of keeping house."

Roosevelt's sister Anna (Bamie) reported that "Theodore did not care for the Marquis, but he was sorry for his wife."

The Marquis told a reporter, "She regrets neither the soft skies of Cannes nor the gilded salons of New York." That was his view. What she actually thought of the badlands is less clear.

How Did Roosevelt Become a Conservationist?

Roosevelt was an avid naturalist from his childhood on. From an early age he studied all creatures great and small, kept specimens in the family's ice box, mastered taxidermy, and he opened the "Roosevelt Museum of Natural History" in his room at the family home on Broadway and Fourteenth Street. Although he killed more than his share of big game in the course of his life, he was at least as interested in the flora and fauna of America from an amateur scientist's and nature lover's point of view as he was in collecting trophies. Prodigious as was his kill list, he never failed to condemn the wanton slaughter of wild animals. He had a particular detestation of what he called "game butchers."

During his badlands years, Roosevelt learned three essential conservation lessons. First, he learned that some animals, once regarded as so abundant as to be an inexhaustible resource, had actually declined in numbers to the point that their very existence was endangered. This was particularly the case with respect to the buffalo (bison).

Roosevelt actually predicted that the buffalo would become extinct. Fortunately, and partly thanks to his efforts, his prediction proved to be erroneous. Roosevelt understood that without concerted efforts to preserve the last herds, preferably by volunteer organizations, but by government when deemed necessary, such creatures were likely to disappear forever. Roosevelt was not afraid to use government as a conservation tool. In fact, he became the greatest conservationist in Presidential history.

Roosevelt saw such animals as the buffalo and the grizzly bear as not only intrinsically fascinating and worth saving, but he also realized that they symbolized both the health of what came to be called ecosystems and the frontier heritage of the American West.

After killing one of the last specimens of the great western buffalo herd in 1883, Roosevelt became an advocate for the preservation and restoration of the buffalo and, as President, helped to create several national bison preserves, including the National Bison Range in northwestern Montana (1909), and what was then Sullys Hill National Park in North Dakota.

Second, particularly after the disastrous winter of 1886-87 on the northern Great Plains, Roosevelt realized that it was quite possible for westerners, including well-meaning cattlemen, to exceed the carrying capacity of the lands on which they lived. Even before the killing winter Roosevelt warned that too many cattle had been crowded onto the Great Plains, that the grasses had been overgrazed, and that any significant disruption of typical grazing conditions was likely to lead to an environmental and economic disaster. This was a key discovery: Roosevelt realized that for all of its ruggedness, the West was a fragile place.

Third, Roosevelt realized that the once-infinite wilderness had been encroached on from all directions, and that only a small remnant of Daniel Boone's primordial America remained. He came to believe that some few particularly magnificent, forbidding, or historically important places should be set aside forever as sanctuaries for the human spirit and monuments to the frontier experience. In other words, his later Presidential achievement of designating 230,000,000 acres of the public domain as federally protected National Forests, National Parks, Federal Bird Sanctuaries (National Wildlife Refuges), National Game Preserves and National Monuments, had roots in his experience in Dakota Territory.

In short, Roosevelt came out of the badlands well aware that the American West was in danger. He realized that leaders (writers, politicians, philanthropists, activists) like himself needed to raise the consciousness of the American public about the threat to their national heritage. And he realized that government must play a role in protecting the natural environment from those who would skim it for easy profits. Roosevelt turned to government regulation not with alacrity, but with his characteristic confidence in the power of government to serve the best interests of the American people.

Roosevelt's first act was to collaborate with like-minded individuals to form a conservation organization, the purpose of which was to insure that his was not the last generation that would experience the joy, adventure, and spiritual renewal of wilderness hunting. In December 1887, Roosevelt invited a dozen influential animal lovers to dine with him at 689 Madison Avenue in New York. Chief among them was George Bird Grinnell, the editor of *Forest and Stream*, who had written a complimentary but not altogether uncritical review of

Roosevelt's *Hunting Trips of a Ranchman*. They discussed the idea of forming an organization of "American hunting riflemen" to work in the public and private sectors to preserve America's natural resources, particularly big game.

The Boone and Crockett Club was founded in January 1888. Its first president was Theodore Roosevelt. It was named for two of Roosevelt's heroes, Daniel Boone (1734-1820) and Davy Crockett (1786-1836). Among other things, the Boone and Crockett Club played an important role in protecting Yellowstone National Park from adverse economic development in the 1890s. The club still exists today. It continues to promote ethical hunting, habitat conservation, and the legacy of Theodore Roosevelt.

Most of the time, Roosevelt was a conservationist not a preservationist. Guided by his tutor in resource management Gifford Pinchot, Roosevelt believed that the nation's goal should be to welcome economic activity and encourage development of our natural resources, but to insist that it be done in a way that was sustainable for future generations, not extractive for short-term profits. Roosevelt agreed that some few sublime or fragile places should be set aside as inviolable forever, but most of the public domain should be open to the maximum sustained yield of its trees, grasses, water, and other resources. Roosevelt admired the great preservationist John Muir, celebrated his uncompromising love of nature, and camped with him as President in 1903 in Yosemite National Park, but he did not always agree with Muir's view that large portions of the West should be protected forever from human economic activity.

What is the Theodore Roosevelt Center?

Dickinson State University is a small state uni-
ersity located on the edge of the North Dakota
adlands that had such a profound influence on
e character and outlook of Theodore Roosevelt.
oosevelt's first home, of course, was Sagamore
ill on Long Island, but his second home—by any
tional measure—was in the Little Missouri River
alley at the western edge of Dakota Territory.

Dickinson State University has embarked upon
n audacious initiative to create—in Roosevelt's
eloved western North Dakota—a national
heodore Roosevelt Center, the foundation of
hich will be a comprehensive digitization of every
nown Roosevelt document. DSU has entered into
formal agreement with the Library of Congress to
igitize its extensive holdings—including more
an 500,000 documents, photographs, illustra-
ons, cartoons, scrapbooks, and film clips. The first
reat phase of that work will be completed late in
008. A formal stakeholders group has been assem-
led, including the Theodore Roosevelt Medora
oundation, Theodore Roosevelt National Park,
e State Historical Society of North Dakota, and
e North Dakota Cowboy Hall of Fame.

The Theodore Roosevelt Center already exists in
modest fashion on the campus of Dickinson State
niversity. With seed money from the U.S.
ongress, the North Dakota State Legislature, and
rivate individuals, a corner of the existing Stoxen
ibrary has been dedicated to the Roosevelt
enter's startup activities. A Web site,
ww.theodorerooseveltcenter.com, is the portal
o DSU's Roosevelt initiatives. Remote kiosks have
een located in the interpretive center at Theodore
oosevelt National Park in Medora and at the
owman, North Dakota, Regional Public Library.

The Theodore Roosevelt Center will be a museum, a traditional Roosevelt library, a comprehensive virtual library, a convening and research center, and the coordinating institution for annual national Theodore Roosevelt symposiums.

Dickinson State University is seeking additional funds from the U.S. Congress, and from the North Dakota State Legislature, which has been asked to fund a large addition to DSU's Stoxen Library, approximately 4,800 square feet of which will be dedicated to the Theodore Roosevelt Center.

Although DSU is a comparatively modest public university, located far from the traditional corridors of the east-coast academic establishment, the information revolution has made it possible for us to undertake this important, nationally significant, and audacious project. We feel that it is wonderfully appropriate that the Theodore Roosevelt Center will be located in Roosevelt's Dakota. "Here," he said in Medora in 1900, "the romance of my life began."

With your help, and some Rooseveltian pluck, we expect to achieve this great and important dream.

Clay S. Jenkinson

What Are the Most Rooseveltian Places in North Dakota?

The most Rooseveltian place in North Dakota is the Elkhorn Ranch site 35 miles north of Medora. Roosevelt chose the site, named the ranch, and thereafter spent most of his time in the Dakota badlands at the Elkhorn, not the Maltese Cross. The Elkhorn Ranch is a national shrine to one of America's greatest Presidents, and one of its supreme conservationists. It's as important as Walden Pond or Thomas Jefferson's Monticello.

The second most Rooseveltian place in North Dakota is the mouth of Cherry Creek in McKenzie County, a few miles east of the north unit of Theodore Roosevelt National Park. It was there, on April 1, 1886, that Roosevelt apprehended the three ruffians who had stolen his boat at the Elkhorn Ranch site and were trying to float downriver out of the badlands country. Surely the adventure with the boat thieves was the most dramatic, indeed heroic, experience Roosevelt had in Dakota Territory. The "arrest" of the thieves at the mouth of Cherry Creek was the stuff of a dime novel or a classic western movie. More than any other event, the boat thieves incident dispelled any notion that Roosevelt was an eastern dude dabbling for a short time on the western frontier. If the rush up Kettle (and San Juan) Hill in Cuba was for Roosevelt "the great day of my life," the adventure with the boat thieves was Roosevelt's great day in Dakota.

The third great site is the place where Roosevelt killed his first buffalo on September 20, 1883. The kill site is actually just inside Montana on upper Little Cannonball Creek. Roosevelt came to Dakota Territory for the express purpose of killing a buffalo. His guide Joe Ferris had expected that they would find a buffalo east of the Little Missouri River. After more than a week of hunting east of the river, Ferris and Roosevelt ventured west towards Montana on September 20, and Roosevelt shot his buffalo later that day. In celebration he did an "Indian war dance" around the carcass, and gave Joe Ferris $100 on the spot.

Dickinson played a key role in Roosevelt's Dakota sojourn on two occasions. It was to Dickinson that he marched the boat thieves on April 11, 1886. When he turned them in to the local sheriff, he received $50, part of it his reward, part reimbursement for the mileage over which he had marched the ruffians. A few months later, on July 4, 1886, Roosevelt delivered a patriotic address in Dickinson. The speech, in which Roosevelt said, "like all Americans I like big things," and, "I am proud indeed to be considered one of yourselves," is regarded as one of Roosevelt's greatest public addresses. In a sense, it might be regarded as his first great national oration. It showed, among other things, that Roosevelt was ready to leave the badlands of Dakota and go back east to take on the world.

Wibaux (then Mingusville) just inside Montana, played an important role in Roosevelt's badlands experience. It was there that he knocked out a gunslinger in the saloon of Nolan's Hotel. When accounts of his bravery spread, it was impossible any longer to dismiss Roosevelt as an eastern dandy. That story found its way into Roosevelt's *Autobiography*. It is a central episode of the Roosevelt legend.

Roosevelt made his decision to invest in the Dakota ranch industry at the cabin of Gregor Lang, at the confluence of Little Cannonball Creek and the Little Missouri River, fifty miles south of the village of Little Missouri. The Lang cabin was TR's headquarters for his buffalo hunt. He shocked everyone by hunting in bad weather all day, for ten days straight, and then sitting up at night talking with Gregor Lang about the West, the cattle industry, and American ideals and politics. It was at the confluence of the Little Cannonball and the Little Missouri that Roosevelt made one of the most momentous decisions of his life—to invest in the Dakota cattle industry and to make "ranching my regular business." He and the Langs formed a lasting friendship, later described with grace by Lincoln Lang in *Ranching with Roosevelt.*

Roosevelt's first Dakota ranch was the Maltese Cross, in the shadow of Chimney Butte. It was there, too, that he spent his first true night in the badlands, September 8, 1883, with Joe Ferris, on his way to the buffalo hunt. It was there that he bought his first badlands horse Nell—because Bill Merrifield and Sylvane Ferris refused to loan or rent him a horse. Soon enough he bought the ranch from its absentee owners and made it his headquarters for his cattle investments.

Further Reading:

Chester L. Brooks and Ray H. Mattison. *Theodore Roosevelt and the Dakota Badlands.* 1958. A reliable short treatment. Particularly good on the world TR found in the badlands.

Michael Collins. *That Damned Cowboy: Theodore Roosevelt and the American West, 1883-1898.* 1990. A good, often original, summary of TR's western adventures.

Hermann Hagedorn. *Roosevelt in the Badlands.* 1921. Still the best one-volume account, slightly marred by Hagedorn's decision to disguise some of the names of TR's acquaintances in the badlands.

Lincoln Lang. *Ranching with Roosevelt.* 1926. A fascinating accounting of the lure of the badlands and Roosevelt's time in North Dakota by a young admirer.

David McCullough. *Mornings on Horseback.* 1981. An excellent study of the Roosevelt family. A bit spotty on TR in Dakota.

Mattison. *"Roosevelt and the Stockgrowers Association." North Dakota History 17.* 1950.

Edmund Morris. *The Rise of Theodore Roosevelt.* 1979. This is one of the best biographies in American history. It won the Pulitzer Prize. It takes TR to the eve of his Presidency.

Carleton Putnam. *Theodore Roosevelt: The Formative Years.* 1958. Without question, the best study of Roosevelt's pre-Presidential years, and the most accurate account of his time in Dakota.

Theodore Roosevelt. *Theodore Roosevelt: An Autobiography.* 1913. TR's autobiography is regarded by historians as one of the two or three best Presidential memoirs.

Jim Vivian. *The Romance of My Life: Theodore Roosevelt's Speeches in Dakota.* 1989. This is a compilation of most of Roosevelt's speeches delivered in northern Dakota Territory and, later, North Dakota. It includes excellent prefatory notes for each speech.

Who Is Clay S. Jenkinson?

Clay S. Jenkinson is the Theodore Roosevelt Scholar-in-Residence at Dickinson State University and the director of the Theodore Roosevelt Center. A Rhodes and Danforth scholar, he studied English language and literature at the University of Minnesota and Oxford University.

Jenkinson is the author of six books, two on Thomas Jefferson, three on the Lewis and Clark Expedition, and a collection of essays entitled *Message on the Wind: A Spiritual Odyssey on the Northern Plains.*

Jenkinson grew up in Dickinson, North Dakota. After living away twenty years in Colorado and Nevada, he returned to North Dakota in 2005.

Clay is considered the nation's foremost first-person interpreter of Thomas Jefferson, Meriwether Lewis, J. Robert Oppenheimer, and Theodore Roosevelt.

Clay is the father of one child, Catherine Missouri, named for the Little Missouri River, the place Clay considers his true home.

In 2006 Clay hiked the Little Missouri River from Marmarth, North Dakota, to the north unit of Theodore Roosevelt National Park, a distance of 173 river miles. The trek took 17 days. For two nights he slept within the perimeter of Roosevelt's Elkhorn Ranch house.

Photo Credits

Theodore Roosevelt Collection, Harvard College Library

Pages 6, 41, 55, 69, 74-75, 77

State Historical Society of North Dakota

Pages 10 ***0410-061,*** 16-17 ***D0471***, 25 ***0200_5x7-764***, ***0098-023***, ***0042-029***, 27 ***0098-023***, 30-31 ***B0437***, 46-47 ***0780***, 58 ***C1451***, 67 ***B0483***, 80 ***0097-07***, 81 ***0042-156,*** ***D0471 0042-156,*** 86-87 ***0410-173,*** 101 ***0739-v1-p31,*** 104 ***SHSND 1972.1630***